2-

To Jay

Sometime the [illegible]

[signature]

THE
IMPACT ZONE

THE
IMPACT ZONE

MASTERING GOLF'S MOMENT OF TRUTH

Bobby Clampett and Andy Brumer

THOMAS DUNNE BOOKS
ST. MARTIN'S PRESS ≈ NEW YORK

THOMAS DUNNE BOOKS.
An imprint of St. Martin's Press.

www.thomasdunnebooks.com
www.stmartins.com

Book design by Maura Fadden Rosenthal/Mspace

Library of Congress Cataloging-in-Publication Data

Clampett, Bobby.
    The impact zone : mastering golf's moment of truth / Bobby
    Clampett and Andy Brumer. — 1st ed.
        p.   cm.
    ISBN-13: 978-0-312-35481-7
    ISBN-10: 0-312-35481-9
    1. Swing (Golf).   I. Brumer, Andy.   II. Title.
    GV979.S9C53 2007
    796.352'3—dc22
                                                2006038715

10   9   8   7

BOBBY CLAMPETT WISHES TO DEDICATE THIS BOOK:

To my wife, Marianna,

and my mother, Jacqueline,

for their steadfast love and encouragement.

CONTENTS

ACKNOWLEDGMENTS

The authors would like to thank several people who contributed significantly to the idea, development, and completion of this book.

Bobby Clampett would like to thank his very first two golf instructors, Lee Martin and Ben Doyle, as well as Wally Goodwin, his high school golf coach at Robert Louis Stevenson High School in Pebble Beach, California, and Karl Tucker, his college golf coach at Brigham Young University. Bobby remains grateful to teaching pros Dave Rasmussen, Rick Smith, Chuck Evans, and others, who worked with him on his swing at various junctures after he turned pro. He's appreciative of the members of the St. David's High School golf team in Raleigh, North Carolina, and several members at Brier Creek Country Club, also in Raleigh, who, in allowing Bobby to work with them on the impact zone's five dynamics, helped him find better ways to communicate their essence to this book's readers. He would also like to thank the entire CBS Sports golf team, with whom he works as a television golf commentator. In addition to his wife, Marianna, and his mother, Jacqueline, to whom he dedicates this book, Bobby wishes to acknowledge all of his children, including his godson, Landon Wiggs, and appreciates their patience, not only during his work on this book but always.

Andy Brumer would like to thank his golf instructor, Gregg McHatton, who helped him clarify and deepen his understanding and execution of the golf swing. He's grateful to the staff at Angeles National Golf Club, in Sunland, California, for their interest in and support of this project. Andy also wishes to remember his late father, Henry Brumer, who always said, "If you can hit it well on the range, you can hit it well on the course," as well as

Adelaida Lopez and Karen Brumer, for their love and their confidence in him as a writer.

Bobby and Andy together wish to acknowledge the late Homer and Sally Kelley: Homer for writing *The Golfing Machine* and Sally for single-handedly keeping the book in circulation for so many years. Kerry Corcoran did a wonderful job capturing Bobby's swing dynamics and instruction during a full day of photography at the Grand Golf Club in San Diego, which graciously and generously offered their beautiful course as backdrop for the shoot. Warren Keating shared his abundant artistic and technical talents in tirelessly transforming the Swing Vision video footage of PGA Tour players into still photographs for the book. Finally the authors wish to thank their agent, John Monteleone, who represented them with friendliness and professionalism, as well as Associate Publisher Peter Wolverton and Associate Editor Katie Gilligan at Thomas Dunne Books, whose faith in the project from the beginning and steady guidance through the publishing process made the writing of this book a pleasure for both.

THE
IMPACT ZONE

INTRODUCTION

You've probably heard that the most important six inches in golf is between the ears. Though the mind unquestionably plays a key role in the game, the most important six inches in the swing truly take place through the *Impact Zone*—meaning the two inches before impact through the four inches after it. After all, they don't call impact the golf swing's Moment of Truth for no reason.

The Impact Zone represents a unique golf instructional book, in that everything in it either focuses on or applies itself to improving a golfer's understanding and execution of impact. Even though top instructors and players unanimously agree on proper impact's supreme status, no one has built an instructional book around it, until now. In other words, here, for the first time, golfers have a book that focuses their attention on the same region of the swing on which the game's greatest players concentrate.

But there's something else that makes this book unique. Most of today's golf instruction, either in printed form or administered on the lesson tee, emphasizes swing style over swing dynamics. By "style" I mean: Does the teacher advocate that both knees stay bent throughout the whole swing; or should the back knee straighten at the top of the swing and the front knee straighten at impact? How much should the head move behind the ball on the backswing? Should golfers swing their hands into a high upright position both at the top of the backswing and at the finish, or should the swing have a flatter or rounder look? How does the club shaft relate to the plane? Is a weak grip better than a strong grip? Where does the toe of the club point at the top of the swing? Does it face the sky in what is called a "closed" position, or drop straight down in an open one? Does the body pivot swing the arms, or do the arms and hands dictate the motion of the body's turning action? What is the proper position of the right arm throughout the swing? And the list goes on and on!

Even advocating a slow, smooth rhythm and tempo over a fast one is an example of style-based instructional bias. Simply put, "style" concerns itself with a series of static, locatable positions or dots that a golfer connects through his or her swing, while "dynamics" involves the efficient creation, storage, and application of power to the ball via a swing whose wholeness transcends the sum of its parts.

My work as a CBS golf commentator has taught me much. I've been witness to the greatest golfer to ever play the game, Tiger Woods. Even though he is only thirty as I write this, it is fair to say that no one in the history of the game has played at his level for a ten-year period. My job requires that I study this phenomenal player and analyze what makes him tick. Studying his game has provided me more evidence that swing-style improvements really do not make for better golf.

Case in point, Tiger has now won major championships with three separate swing styles. In 1997 he won the Masters by twelve strokes with a swing that was steep in the middle, the club face shut and crossing the line at the top. In 2000 he won the U.S. Open by fifteen strokes, with a swing that was on a more conventional plane, with a squared club face, while, in 2005, he won two major championships with a club shaft slightly laid off, or flat, in the middle of his backswing, meaning that it pointed slightly to the right of his ball-to-target line than would a technically on-plane backswing. He has also worked on other swing-style changes that perhaps we'll discuss more in a second book. But one thing that has remained consistent in Tiger's game is his ability to maintain his wonderful swing dynamics. He has never replaced dynamics with style, but has changed his style while maintaining his dynamics.

While style has its place in playing good golf, it pales in comparison with working on dynamics. In fact, when I went out on the PGA Tour in 1980 I had excellent dynamics, packaged in my own individualized style. I'm certain now, had I continued to focus on improving those dynamics as I learned them from my childhood golf teacher, Ben Doyle, I would have had a better playing career. Instead, I listened to too-many style-oriented instructors, voices that were being heard everywhere on tours, men who were popular among players, starting in the mid-1980s.

These guys told me things like "You're taking the club back too far to the inside," or "Your club face is too shut at the top." One top teacher said that my swing had "more moving parts than an erector set." Another had the gall to tell me that I had to "forget everything I ever learned or knew about the golf swing" before he would agree to work with me. Talk about narrow-minded arrogance! Yet, the same scenario continually plays itself out with average players, and, obviously, average teachers on driving ranges, golf courses, and country clubs everywhere.

My game deteriorated as my focus shifted to style changes. I changed my grip, my stance, my backswing, and yes, even my downswing and finish. My swing became golf's version of connect the dots, with each dot representing a static position. My feel for my dynamics was gone, and so was my playing career.

I believe golfers will learn to strike the ball solidly through the impact zone by developing and improving the five essential dynamics of the golf swing that they will learn in this book. These dynamics all work together to create a unified and whole motion. You will learn these dynamics by beginning with the putt, then progressing to the chip, and then the pitch shot, before concluding with the full swing.

Dynamic #1: *Putting: The Flat Left Wrist at Impact.* You will see that, when you putt, you want to strike the ball with a flat left wrist. This insures that the club and the left arm and wrist move at the same pace and speed through the impact zone. A flat left wrist also provides the structure you need to withstand the force of impact, which, while minimal when putting, becomes quite considerable with full shots.

Dynamic #2: *Chipping: The Forward Swing Bottom.* As you progress from the putt to the chip, you will see that that same flat left wrist allows you to strike down and through the ball, with a forward swing bottom whose divot is ideally four to five inches in front of the ball. As you shall see when players achieve a successful forward swing bottom, their ball striking improves immediately and immeasurably.

Dynamic #3: *Pitching: Loading the Club on the Backswing.* In order to apply power to the ball through the impact zone, you first have to establish the physics of power on the backswing. I call this "loading," and you create it via a cocking of the left wrist in conjunction with the body's backswing, or pivot coil, so that the entire backswing is a continuous and fluid "loading" motion.

Dynamic #4: *Swinging: Lagging the Load Through the Impact Zone.* Once you've successfully loaded the club with power, you have to preserve or store that power until the very last second, when you apply it into the ball. That conservation process is called "lag," and without it, good golf is virtually impossible. In short, load your lag during the backswing, and lag your load during the downswing through the impact zone.

Dynamic #5: *Swinging the Club Along a Straight Plane Line Through the Impact Zone.* Golf is a target game, therefore, you have to direct your club efficiently—now loaded with lagged power—toward your target. In other words, you have to have all of your energy oriented in one direction, on a straight plane line, as you swing the club through the impact zone.

We will devote a chapter to the importance of playing with the proper equipment that complements your swing and works to maximize your swing dynamics. It will become clear that using ill-fitted gear can be a golfer's worst enemy, and that doing so can break down each and every one of your coveted swing dynamics.

"Mental Dynamics," the concluding chapter, will focus on a mental approach to golf, but not one that readers have encountered before in the countless pop psychology, self-help, "mental game" golf books. In other words, rather than talking about developing confidence in one's swing, a repeating preshot routine, and a "one shot at a time" attitude, as many of these books do, this chapter will help you visualize and mentally conceptualize all of the swing dynamics into a unified whole, so that ultimately, you are no longer burdened with swing "thoughts" out on the course, but have a clear picture of how to dynamically deliver the club through the impact zone. In this chapter I will also review the five swing dynamics and how to practice them in a time-effective, efficient, and enjoyable manner.

There's something else that's very exciting and unique about this book, and that is our use of the extremely slow motion Swing Vision camera, the one that you see on our CBS telecasts capturing the swings of PGA Tour players through the impact zone. We were able to convert the video to still images, and the information these pictures reveal is as astounding as it is instructional. Even if there have been similar photos of impact transferred from video, no book has visually explored the impact zone of the world's greatest players as closely and authentically as this one.

Among the things you will see is that the overwhelming majority of these great players strike slightly down on the ball through the impact zone with their drivers. You'll also see that their swing bottoms, with irons and woods, fall a good four inches in front of the ball.

The dialog, which I've presented as a *duel* between style and dynamics, is anything but new. Think about Jack Nicklaus's swing, which the stylists ridiculed when he arrived on tour, because of its unconventional flying right elbow. Lee Trevino, considered along with Ben Hogan as the modern game's premier ball striker, had a thoroughly unorthodox and original swing. While the golf pundits said that no one else should ever try to copy Lee's swing, today one that mirrors his swing, i.e., with a backswing outside of the line and a downswing looped back to the inside, has become the conventional way most tour pros play, and how many top teachers teach the swing. It obviously took some time before the golf experts saw past Lee's style and into the heart of his fabulous dynamics!

There's more. Corey Pavin and Johnny Miller had very weak grips, Hubert Green and Fuzzy Zoeller had very low hands at address, while Mo Norman and Wayne Levi had their hands so high at address that their left wrists were completely level, if not a little arched down. Numerous players, such as Kenny Perry, Jay Haas, Michelle Wie, Hale Irwin, Corey Pavin, and Johnny Miller, set and load the club early on the backswing. Greats like Nicklaus and the late Payne Stewart had a very late backswing set and load, while innumerable stars, Tiger Woods, Greg Norman, and Annika Sorenstam among them, set and load gradually, at different points in their backswings.

With all of this in mind, I'd like to tell you a story about my own experimentation, and a dynamic discovery from which the idea for this book sprung. It was late in 1980. I had just turned pro and began playing on the PGA Tour, when, suddenly, I found that I had inexplicably lost that wonderful feeling of hitting a perfectly struck golf shot. As my distance and accuracy decreased, I knew instinctively that I'd have to find a way to return to the simple basics in executing the fundamentals of hitting the ball solidly. I had read somewhere that when Ben Hogan struggled with his game (yes, even Hogan struggled!), he would go into a room and sit all day alone with a golf club in his hand and just think about what was wrong with his swing. My sanctuary for thought turned out to be a secluded corner on the grounds at Pinehurst, in North Carolina, not far from where I now live, during a tournament called the Hall of Fame Classic. There, all alone among a shady grove of pine trees, out of sight from my fellow tour pros, I began making practice swings with a 5-iron, and without a ball, down and through the sandy soil.

After several swings I began to notice that my divots, taken out of Pinehurst's soft and sandy soil, began either right where I would have positioned my ball or a little behind that spot. The latter was a bright red flag of warning, which immediately told me that I wasn't catching the ball with a proper descending blow. In other words, I was hitting the turf just prior to the ball at impact, and because the club immediately began to swing up and in, right after reaching the low or bottom point of its arc, I was losing both power and control on my actual shots.

So, I returned right then and there to the aiming point concept that I had learned from Homer Kelley's *The Golfing Machine,* as Ben Doyle taught it to me on the range at Quail Lodge in Carmel Valley, California. In fact, several of the concepts and fundamentals I discuss in this book come from that book, and I owe it, and Ben, a public acknowledgment and a nod of gratitude.

This "aiming point" technique involves drawing an imaginary line from the hands, at the top of the backswing, to a point in front of the ball along the ball-to-target line, which, in fact, forms the Fifth Dynamic, "The Straight Plane Line." As the backswing transitions to the downswing, the golfer directs or "aims" his or her hands, not at the ball, but at that point in front of the ball.

Just a swing or two using the aiming point technique moved my divots instantly forward, and, with a blend of relief and hopeful anticipation, I headed back to the practice range and began applying the technique to hitting real balls.

I immediately struck the ball more solidly than I had been in the previous weeks, but what I really found exhilarating was the accompanying sensation of unencumbered freedom and speed with which my club swung through the ball, all the way to the finish of the swing. I noticed the bottom or deepest points of my divots now lay four to five inches in front of the ball, with the divot starting at or slightly in front of the ball every time. Though this occurred at the tail end of the 1980 season, this finding proved to be my launchpad for the 1981 season. It was no wonder that I finished in the top twenty on the PGA Tour money list those two seasons.

Learning to strike the ball first this way, with an on-plane club path that continues downward and forward after impact, will form the cornerstone on which this book is based.

Unfortunately, though I had righted my listing ship via the sand drill, I nevertheless (and, perhaps, unknowingly) contracted that germ, on tour known as "rabbit ears," which compels championship-level golfers to distrust their instincts and listen to any ruddy-faced, gold-braceleted teaching pro with even a modicum of a reputation—someone who, with the swagger of a used car salesman, tries to convince you that he will improve your swing. So I snatched defeat out of the jaws of victory—and began "working" with several of these pros; and I saw my dynamics fade away again, along with the improvement I had achieved from my drills in the sand. In my pursuit of improving my swing style, I lost sight of my dynamics and fell into that deep chasm of missed cuts and return visits to qualifying school.

It wasn't until I decided to stop playing the tour full-time, after the 1995 PGA Tour season, that my body's muscles were able to fully relax and regain the knowledge that I had regrettably tossed overboard. I quit golf completely for eighteen months so that my muscle memory would forget the poor swing habits I had developed. Slowly, I began to regain trust in my previous conviction that upgraded swing dynamics represented the key to my regaining that form.

Indeed, I had come full circle, and the fruits of that journey ripened in 2000, when I qualified for the U.S. Open at Pebble Beach, finished the first round in fourth place, and wound up in thirty-seventh place at the end of the event. In 2005 I shot 67 in a U.S. Open qualifying round, and were it not for my fabulous job at CBS Sports broadcasting golf on TV, I'd certainly have increased my playing ambitions beyond U.S. Open–qualifying and occasional PGA and European tour events. The point is that I have finally recovered my swing dynamics, and my reinstated, four-inch forward swing bottom is its distinctive signature.

In fact, I have become so enthusiastic over the prospect of helping all golfers to move their swing bottoms four inches forward of the ball, that I did a little detective work just to provide readers with some indisputable evidence that this is indeed an idea whose time has come. My partner in eradicating this crime of insufficiently-forward swing bottoms was my godson Landon Wiggs, a high school student in Raleigh, North Carolina, whom I contracted to conduct a random study of amateur golfers of varying ages and abilities, of both sexes. The objective was to measure their swing bottom and compare it to their handicap. If what I am saying is true, then the more forward one's swing bottom, the better they should play golf.

Landon spent several days over the period of a couple of months compiling a random sample of golfers on the driving range of the Lochmere Golf Club in Cary, North Carolina, a semi-private golf course near Raleigh. Ages ranged from fourteen to midseventies, and each golfer was asked to hit five balls with their 7-iron. The balls were placed in the middle of a line on the grass and the divots taken were evaluated in terms their distance in front of this line. Measurements were taken from the line to the deepest portion of the divot, i.e., the low, or bottom, point of each swing's arc. The best and the worst of the five were thrown out, meaning that only the middle three were measured, then an average of everyone's middle three was taken. The results were amazing, and, I believe, are proof positive that there's a direct correlation between one's handicap or general ability to play the game well and one's swing-bottom location, either behind, directly at, or in front of the ball.

The results are shown in the table on page 10. The swing-bottom numbers are in inches.

The average swing bottom of a PGA Tour professional is four inches in front of the ball, and that is a dramatic differential that exists between them and most amateurs. In fact, the really high-handicap golfers' swing bottoms fall nearly one foot behind the

Results	AVG Handicap	AVG Swing Bottom	Swing-Bottom Range
Men			
PGA Touring Pros	+4 or +5*	+4	+3 to +5
Handicap 0–9	5	+1.6	0 to +3
Handicap 10–19	13.7	−1.92	−5 to 0
Handicap 20–32	25.13	−4.12	−5 to −2
Women			
Women Handicap 8–19	14.38	−2	−4 to +1
Women Handicap 20–45	35.3	−5.14	−6 to −4

*(pros don't have handicaps)

swing bottoms of the pros. How could these amateur players ever hit a solid shot, even off a really high tee? Consider not only the huge loss of power, and of accuracy and consistency, when the golf club bottoms out into the ground well behind the ball, then bounces into the ball on an upward and erratic swing path.

No wonder there are so many frustrated golfers quitting the game every year. What's more, how much help are golfers really getting through technical advances, new equipment, traditional swing instruction, mental coaching, etc.? If we could somehow change the way the game is taught, and begin working from the ground up with a focus of the golfers' swing dynamics, and with the goal of moving their swing bottoms four inches in front of the ball, we could begin to make some real progress—progress that would both grow the game and make it immeasurably more enjoyable for those already hooked on playing it.

Let's look at the numbers a little more closely. With the approximate range of handicaps (forty strokes) and a range of swing bottoms of nine inches between the pros and the high-handicap amateurs, one can deduce that a golfer will reduce his or her average score by four strokes for every forward inch of improvement made on the swing bottom. I've found that in giving a person a fifteen-to-thirty minute lesson that focuses on moving their swing bottoms forward, I can usually improve that swing bottom (i.e., move it forward) by one to three inches. That's four to twelve strokes per round of improvement in less than thirty minutes!

These are the kinds of results for which teaching pros have been searching for years. And reading, studying, and practicing the material presented in this book practically guarantees them. In other words, hope for better golf lies right at your feet, just four inches in front of the ball, to be exact! It is with this optimistic spirit, and the conviction that by improving one's swing dynamics you can improve your game more quickly and soundly than ever before, that I invite you to step with me into *The Impact Zone.*

CHAPTER ONE

PUTTING:

Dynamic #1— The Flat Left Wrist at Impact

The teaching method used in this book mirrors the one employed by the late, legendary instructor Harvey Penick to teach his young student Ben Crenshaw how to play golf. Harvey taught Ben the game's short shots and small swings first, meaning putts, chip shots, and pitches, before moving his future hall of famer on to the irons and woods. In other words, Crenshaw, Tom Kite, and the countless other golfers Mr. Penick taught, learned the game from the green back to the tee, and not the other way around, as most golf pros teach the game today.

My first teacher was Lee Martin, who first taught me to play when I was ten. Lee didn't specifically start me off with the short game, but he did instill in me the importance of developing one as quickly as possible. He did this by giving me daily assignments, to work on my putting, chipping, pitching, and bunker play at the little chipping green that was located next to the first tee at our beautiful course, Carmel Valley Golf and Country Club, which is now called The Quail Lodge Golf Club, in Carmel Valley, California, just a few miles from Pebble Beach.

Soon, the better-playing members at my club, such as John Roberts, would stop by and join me in practice. It was not uncommon for Mr. Roberts (who had been a member of Sciota Country Club in Columbus, Ohio, and watched a promising young junior there named Jack Nicklaus grow up and develop his extraordinary skills) and I to practice for two or three hours on the short game alone. We had a running bet to see who could make a string of the longest running consecutive up and downs from the practice bunker. We would carry a separate bet onto the course and keep tabs on consecutive up and downs from the bunkers. I remember Mr. Roberts once telling me his tally reached the midthirties. Mine never made it past the teens, but I thought that was pretty good at that time.

When minitour players, such as Mark Rolfing, now a golf commentator for NBC Sports, and the now-well-known teaching pro, Jim McLean, came by, we all would have some fun practicing together. I can recall many contests Jim and I would have. I could handle Mr. Roberts pretty regularly by the time I reached fourteen years old, but Jim beat me like a drum. Yet, I gleaned much from watching good players like Jim and Mark. These types of positive relationships helped develop a joy and a purpose when practicing (both the long and the short shots) that I still feel today whenever I work on my game.

When I was fourteen and a freshman at the Robert Louis Stevenson School in Pebble Beach, California, the athletic director, Wally Goodwin (who later became the golf coach at Stanford, where he recruited a pretty good junior named Tiger Woods), asked me to be his partner in the Northern California Best-Ball Championship, played on one of our school's home courses, the legendary Spyglass Hill.

In the opening round I shot an even-par-72, while hitting only six greens in regulation. I couldn't even reach many of the par-4s, such as holes number six, nine, and thirteen, in two shots, though that round alone seemed to have developed my reputation as one of those players to watch on and around the greens. Those who knew me then were never surprised to see me in the top twenty on the PGA Tour money list in my first two years on tour, and my well-practiced short game as a youngster had a lot to do with my early success as a pro.

The reason our book begins with the short game strokes is that the fundamentals of the putt, chip, and pitch shots are the same as those of full swing shots with the irons, metalwood shots, and the driver. Yet, because of their abbreviated length and the relative slow speed at which they are executed, the short game swings are much simpler to learn. Mastering the short game shots forms a foundation on which golfers can build dynamically sound full swings.

We are beginning specifically with putting, because the putting stroke takes place exclusively through the impact zone, i.e., it doesn't require a full backswing, nor a through swing or body pivot. Learning a fundamentally sound golf swing by starting with putting, reflects my belief that the simpler we can make the game, the better off all golfers will be.

As we said in the introduction, *The Impact Zone* will also emphasize dynamics over style. So let's get started with putting, by introducing Dynamic Number One, the Flat Left Wrist at Impact, which will initiate our step-by-step, building block approach to learning each of golf's five dynamics, as they progress to chipping, pitching, and finally the full swing.

The first law of Dynamic Number One is, regardless of the length of shot you are playing, you must arrive at impact with a *flat left wrist.* Look at these photographs of me at impact, while hitting a wedge and a driver. Note in each picture how the left wrist is flat and how the club has a forward lean of the club shaft (though the angle of forward lean varies according to the shot).

Let's now turn your attention to putting, while keeping in mind that this chapter will not serve as an all-encompassing commentary on putting. Rather, it will focus on putting from the perspective of the first dynamic, which will set the tone for you to develop your whole golf game and swing, dynamic by dynamic. I could write a book on putting alone.

Note that at impact my left wrist is flat and the shaft leans forward on both a wedge and a driver shot. (Photos by Kerry Corcoran.)

There have been many great putters throughout the history of the game and virtually all of them have exhibited widely different styles. Isao Aoki from Japan, for instance, simply hinges his wrists back and forth, picks the putter head up, and almost chops down into the ball with a putting stroke that resembles a chip shot. South African Bobby Locke used to, and countryman Gary Player still does putt with a closed stance. Locke aimed right, hooded his putter blade left, and imparted hook spin on his putts. Jack Nicklaus putts with an open stance and moves his right arm straight down the line of the putt, like a piston. Ben Crenshaw blends his shoulder, arm, and hand motions into a fluid and graceful stroke that gradually opens the putter's face on the backstroke then closes it after striking the ball.

Because the rules of golf allow for so many different putting methods, stroking the ball on the green into the hole has become a true art form. For example, the long putter, used today by Bernhard Langer and LPGA player Beth Daniel, among others, has golfers pinch the top of the putter grip with the thumb and forefinger of the left hand, which stays pinned in a stationary fashion against the chest. This allows them to stroke the putter shaft and head back and through the ball with the right hand alone, in a pendulum fashion. Conversely, the newly developed, so-called "claw" grip, employed effectively by Chris DiMarco, Mark Calcavecchia, and countless others, removes the right hand almost completely off the club, which means that the left hand plays a bigger role in stroking the putter back and through.

Let's not forget about the belly putter, also a relatively new method of putting, which roots a longer-than-standard putter into the golfer's navel in order to stabilize the stroke. Fred Couples, known for his folksy, no-nonsense approach to golf, has applied the cross-handed grip with the belly putter method, in a hybrid style that has improved his putting considerably. So, I'm conceding that any style of putting that gets the ball into the hole on the most consistent basis is the one you should adopt.

Now let's work on a three-foot putt.

Dynamic Number One, a Flat Left Wrist, assures (and requires) that your left arm, the back of your left wrist, and the putter shaft form a straight line when you contact the ball. Even on a short putt like this one, which obviously doesn't involve or require a great deal of club head speed, you still generate a significant amount of force when your putter head collides with the ball. Therefore, you need a structurally sound and solid impact position to absorb this blow and to impart energy into the ball in an efficient, consistent, and controlled manner. A flat left wrist at impact provides this for you, and, as I've said (and will repeatedly emphasize), it is the number-one, key alignment for hitting solid golf shots, from the putt to the drive.

Here's a little exercise that will let you both see and sense what a flat left wrist feels like: Take the back of your left hand and lay it flush against a wall. Notice how the back of the hand, wrist, and forearm create, or lie on, a flat, straight plane. Now, remove your arm from the wall and take your normal putting grip on your putter, keeping this straight line between your left arm, the back of your left wrist, and the putter shaft. Extend your arm directly in front of you, so that the club shaft is horizontal to the ground, and you will clearly see this arm/wrist/shaft straight-line configuration. Now simply lower the club to the ground and maneuver yourself into your normal, comfortable putting stance, and you will be in a solid putting setup position. Note that your left hand grip will be considerably weaker (turned to the left) on your putter than when gripping other clubs for full shots.

Because the length of the putting stroke is so short, you don't have time to release the club into a flat left wrist position through the impact zone, as you do on fuller or longer swings. That's why you want a flat left wrist in the impact position, right from the address when putting—again, with the left arm and club shaft forming a straight line down from the left shoulder. In other words, when putting, your impact and address positions are one and the same.

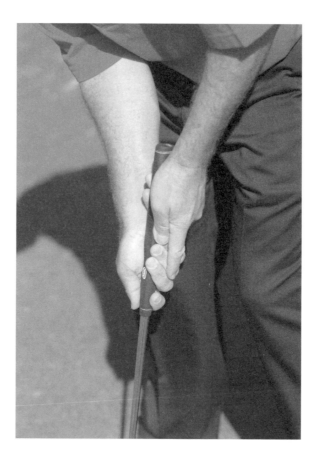

This is a close-up on my putting grip. *(Photo by Kerry Corcoran.)*

To assure that you indeed do have a flat left wrist alignment at address, I want your hands positioned slightly forward of the ball, which will tilt or lean the club shaft slightly forward as well. I've found that positioning the ball two or three inches behind my left heel comfortably creates both a flat left wrist alignment and a forward-leaning club shaft angle at address. You can go as far back with your ball position as the middle of your stance, but any farther forward than, say, two inches behind your left heel position will tend to bend, or cup, your left wrist backwards, as you swing the club head through to reach the ball at impact—and that's the opposite of what you are trying to achieve.

Here's another exercise that clearly illustrates the problem with an excessively forward ball position when putting. From a correct address and impact flat left wrist position, without moving your arms, swing your putter head forward toward your target with your wrists alone. You can see that, as the putter head moves forward, the shaft tilts back and your left wrist cups or bends as well. This kind of breakdown of the flat left wrist is the number-one error golfers make, not only with putting, but with chipping, pitching, and on the full swing. It is the principal culprit that destroys a dynamic impact position and a dynamic swing. I've asked

you to do this little exercise, because feeling what is incorrect vis-a-vis proper technique can help us engrain in ourselves the proper golf fundamentals. Jack Nicklaus has written about how, on the practice range, he would at times purposely swing with faulty fundamentals, to more fully distinguish the feel of good mechanics from bad ones.

I think it's worth pointing out that two of the three styles of putting I mentioned above emphasize the important role of the

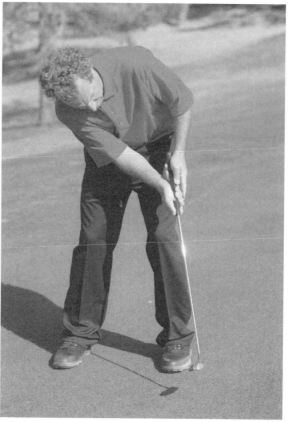

Here I am making a full putting stroke. Note my ball position, about three inches rearward of my left heel, my flat left wrist at impact, and how the putter shaft and my left arm and wrist remain in a straight line throughout the stroke. *(Photos by Kerry Corcoran.)*

flat left wrist at impact when putting, albeit in slightly disguised ways. The long putting method eliminates the possibility of the left wrist breaking down at impact by all but removing the left hand from the club. The claw grip adopts the complete opposite strategy to achieve the same goal. It takes the right hand off the club, which allows the left wrist to remain flat throughout the stroke, without any interference from an overly active right hand.

Note in the pictures above how I start with a flat left wrist at address and maintain the flat left wrist through to the finish, and hold it until the putt drops! *(Photos by Kerry Corcoran.)*

Let's return to making a dynamic putting stroke using the conventional putting grip, with the right hand below the left on the club (for right-handed putters, of course). Now, with your left wrist flat, and the putter shaft and your left wrist and arm all in a straight line, maintain this alignment as you gently rock your shoulders up and down, to make a short backstroke and an accelerating through stroke without moving your body. Think of your arms and shoulders as a triangle that must be kept intact as you rock your shoulders. When stroking the ball, make sure that you maintain the natural bend in the back of your right wrist, well into the follow-through of your stroke. In fact, a bent right wrist and a flat left wrist go hand in hand (no pun intended!).

Unfortunately, the converse is equally true, because, as soon as you begin to straighten or flatten your right wrist during the stroke, your left wrist loses its flatness and immediately begins to bend. Increasing the bend in the right wrist a little on the backstroke will facilitate being able to sustain a flat left wrist on the through stroke. This more sophisticated move in the putting stroke is one that Loren Roberts, "The Boss of the Moss," executes beautifully. He calls this part of his stroke "the little lag move," and, as we'll see, lag is our fourth swing dynamic.

Whether or not you increase the bend in your right wrist on the backstroke, the task in putting is to maintain a flat left wrist and a bent right wrist throughout the entire stroke.

Here's an important grip tip that will help you sustain a flat left wrist through the entire putting stroke, including, of course, the impact zone: Add a little extra pressure in the last three fingers of your left hand, and monitor that pressure, so that it remains constant through the entire stroke.

Your left wrist actually dictates the movement of the putter face and controls the face angle during the stroke, so keeping it flat through impact assures that you will strike the ball with the putter face squarely looking down your intended line. The golf swing functions as a simple machine, and the less moving parts in the machine, the less that can go wrong with your shots. By keeping a flat left wrist when putting, you reduce the number of the machine's moving parts.

Let's look a little more closely at what specifically goes wrong with the putting stroke when the flat left wrist at impact breaks down into a bent or cupped one. First of all, a left wrist that breaks down during the stroke changes the acceleration of the putter, just as it alters the pressure in your grip. A flat left wrist ensures that the putter head and face move at the same rate of speed as the left hand and arm. A cupped left wrist moves the bottom of your putter's swing rearward, and, as it does, it changes the alignment of the club face at impact. In other words, the act of breaking down the flat left wrist during the stroke automatically introduces elements of inconsistency in the stroke, each with its own problem, and each adding up to poor putting. So, let's get rid of all of these problems by establishing a flat left wrist at address, and maintaining it through the backstroke and through the impact zone.

Is there any complex technique or magical secret you should know that will insure that you maintain a flat left wrist throughout the stroke? Mechanically, the above-mentioned rocking motion of the shoulders does wonders in taking independent hand motion out of the stroke and sustaining the essential flat left wrist/bent right wrist combination. Mentally, I want you to simply think about keeping your left wrist flat throughout the stroke. It's amazing what a little mindfulness can do.

Remember, in the introduction I defined a swing dynamic as the efficient creation, storage, and application of power to the ball. The presence of a flat left wrist at impact in the putt, chip, pitch, and full swing allows this to happen efficiently, because it lessens if not eliminates any kind of uneven and erratic motion in the swing. In many ways, the flat left wrist at impact qualifies as golf's master dynamic.

Putting cross-handed, or as it is often called now, "left hand low," works effectively to facilitate a flat left wrist at impact. This style places the left hand below the right and therefore closer to the hole than the right hand, in a strong position to pull the putter through the impact zone, while maintaining a firm and flat left wrist. Bruce Lietzke was the first tour pro I recall seeing putt this way.

Many people know about Bruce's aversion to practice. So, when I saw how well he putted cross-handed, I knew there was something inherently sound in the method, because I reasoned that he surely didn't groove that stroke putting past sunset on the practice green! By putting cross-handed, people thought Bruce (and others, such as Tom Kite, who won the 1992 U.S. Open putting cross-handed) was ostensibly admitting that he wasn't a good putter. Quite to the contrary, Bruce simply found a putting style that helped him produce better impact dynamics.

PGA teaching professional Mike Furyk, Jim Furyk's dad, asked Gary Player about the cross-handed putting method, because he wanted to start his twelve-year-old son Jim, then a beginner, putting this way. Gary said that he would strongly recommend it to anyone just taking up golf. The Black Knight went as far as to say that, were he to do it all over again, he would have begun by putting cross-handed himself. In fact, I think you would see many more tour stars putt cross-handed today, had they not so thoroughly engrained the "conventional" putting grip in their muscle memories through so many years of practice and play. I think all golfers should at least give this grip a try.

Many putter manufacturers, such as Yes Putters (with whom I have a professional relationship), use slow-motion video cameras both in their research and development departments and while fitting golfers for putters. We can observe some interesting things by looking at footage from such cameras, especially about putts, right at and immediately after impact. The first thing that you can see when doing so is that the ball stays on the club face considerably longer when a putt is struck with a flat left wrist, as opposed to a bent left wrist. The physics of the game says that, the longer you can keep the ball on the club face (on all shots), the

more energy the club transfers to the ball; and that translates into more consistently solid contact at impact.

When the left wrist breaks down at impact, instead of the putter face remaining level with the ball and compressing it, the whole club head swings slightly upward. Now the club face contacts the circumference of the ball obliquely, so that the swing path and the ball act like two meshing gears, which means less-than-solid putts.

What's more, the instant the left wrist breaks down, the acceleration rate of the stroke also changes from smooth and steady to flippy, jerky, and erratic. What actually happens is that, the instant the putter head swings past the left arm, it actually slows down in

PGA Tour player Briny Baird demonstrates an effective technique using the cross-handed grip. Note how he creates a flat left wrist at the address position and maintains it throughout the stroke. His choice of a very closed stance is a matter of style. *(Photos by Kerry Corcoran.)*

an attempt to realign itself with the shaft. Again, the result is inconsistent impact. No wonder Lee Trevino said that the number-one fundamental in the golf swing is to keep the flat back of the left wrist and arm accelerating through the impact zone!

Rhythm plays a larger role in putting than people realize, and maintaining a flat left wrist through the putting stroke plays a vital role in putting rhythmically. Here's how it works: The flat left wrist acts as a gate that allows a stroke's rear and forward halves to swing in an even and rhythmic fashion, back and through the impact zone. It's a bit ironic that perhaps the best model for a flat left wrist at impact when putting is Phil Mickelson's flat right wrist, because Phil putts left-handed. Yet, if we were to watch Phil putt in a mirror, or reverse his stroke on tape or in a sequence of photographs, we would see him lock his "left" wrist in a flat position at address, then keep it there throughout the backstroke and right through the impact zone. Loren Roberts is another great putting model, since you can clearly see that his left arm and putter move at the exact same speed and pace throughout his stroke. Loren can thank his flat left wrist at impact for this.

DYNAMIC PUTTING DRILLS

1. THE "LEFT-RIGHT-BOTH" DRILL

First the golfer will hit a putt with his or her left arm and hand only, striving for a flat left wrist through the entire stroke, including, of course, the impact zone. Next, the golfer will hit a putt with the right hand and arm only, keeping the right wrist bent through impact (which automatically creates a flat left wrist). Finally, the golfer will putt with both hands on the grip, feeling the flat left wrist and the bent right wrist work as a team to create solid putts through the impact zone. During steps one and three of this drill, the golfer will monitor the grip pressure in the last

three fingers of the left hand, and notice that increasing that pressure helps to maintain a flat left wrist.

2. The Putting Gate Drill

This drill asks golfers to build a gate, using two tees that straddle the line of their putt just in front of the ball. The golfer places the two tees about three to four inches apart and three to six feet in front of the ball. He or she then putts balls through this gate, while maintaining a flat left wrist throughout the entire stroke.

Pages 29-30: Putting with the left hand alone is a great way to learn the mechanics and feel of a flat left wrist at impact. *(Photos by Kerry Corcoran.)*

3. The Bowling Alley Drill

The golfer will place a small coin four to six feet in front of the ball and practice putting the ball over the coin, while keeping the image of a flat left wrist and a bent right wrist in his or her mind. This is a great drill to do indoors, when you can find the right type of carpet that simulates a putting green.

4. The Antidribble Drill

This drill requires the golfer to strike thirty-to-fifty-foot putts, and to pay specific attention to how much the ball is airborne, or bounces off the green soon after impact. A bouncing ball can be caused by the golfer striking the ball with either too much or too little loft. The golfer must pay close attention to whether impact is causing the ball to ride or lift on top of the green, and initially skid for too long, or if impact is causing the ball to pound into the green and bounce immediately off the putter face. The golfer will monitor his or her ball placement and make slight stance adjustments, forward or backward, so as to achieve optimum ball roll. He or she will also pay attention to which ball position best sustains the coveted flat left wrist/bent right wrist combination throughout the stroke, and especially through the impact zone. The less the ball bounces off the putter face, the better the speed of the putt, which means improved distance control, better lag putts, and more putts sunk. If all ball positions produce skidding or bouncing putts, the golfer should experiment with increasing or reducing the loft on their putter.

BULLET POINTS

- The fundamentals of the putt, chip, and pitch shots are the same as those of full swing shots with the irons, fairway metal-wood shots, and the driver, therefore, mastering the short game shots forms a foundation on which golfers can build dynamically sound full swings.

- Take the back of your left hand and lay it flush against a wall. Notice how the back of the hand, wrist, and the forearm create, or lie on, a flat, straight plane. Now, remove your arm from the wall and take your normal putting grip on your putter, keeping intact this straight line between your left arm, the back of your left wrist, and now the putter shaft. Extend your arm directly in front of you, so that the club shaft is horizontal to the ground, and you will clearly see this arm/wrist/shaft straight-line configuration. Now, simply lower the club to the ground and maneuver yourself into your normal comfortable putting stance and you will be in a solid putting setup position.

- Think of your arms and shoulders as a triangle that must be kept intact as you rock your shoulders. When stroking the ball, make sure that you maintain the natural bend in the back of your right wrist, well into the follow-through of your stroke. In fact, a bent right wrist and flat left wrist go hand in hand.

- A flat left wrist insures that the putter head and face move at the same rhythmic rate of speed as the left hand and arm. A cupped left wrist moves the bottom of your putter's swing rearward, and as it does it changes the alignment of the club face at impact and automatically introduces many elements of incon-sistency to the stroke.

• Because it lessens if not eliminates any kind of uneven and er-ratic motion in the swing, the flat left wrist at impact qualifies as golf's master dynamic.

CHAPTER TWO

CHIPPING:

Dynamic #2—
The Forward Swing Bottom
(The Aiming Point Technique,
and the Sand Drill)

Now that you've learned the golf swing's first dynamic, the flat left wrist at impact, in the case of the putting stroke, you can move on to the second stage, chipping, and Dynamic Number Two, which is the Forward Swing Bottom. This includes the aiming point technique and the all-important sand drill.

As the putting stroke lengthens into a chipping stroke, your goal changes in one significant way: Rather than rolling the ball with your putting stroke smoothly along the ground, with minimum backspin or maximum overspin (meaning the least amount of bounce and/or skid), the chip requires you to hit the ball into the air, which creates backspin on the golf ball. The only way you can accomplish this is to strike down on the ball with an accelerating stroke, so that the bottom, or center of the swing arc, as well as the divot, falls approximately four inches in front of the ball. In other words, during the chipping stroke, the club moves downward and strikes the ball before it reaches both the ground and the bottom of its arc. It then continues to descend to its low point of four inches in front of the ball, before it swings back up to complete the stroke. This low point, which identifies the center of your divot, is literally what the second dynamic, a forward swing bottom, means.

Because a chip shot resembles a putt in that it is a small stroke (with little wrist hinging and unhinging back and through), you want to maintain a flat left wrist throughout the stroke, and of course through the impact zone, just as you did while putting. Therefore, you will address the chip with your left wrist in a flat position, in the same manner as you did with your putting stroke.

PGA Tour pro Chris Couch uses the cross-handed, left-hand-low grip when chipping, to ensure his left wrist remains flat at impact. While such a grip may not be for everyone, it sure worked well when he chipped in on the final hole, to win the 2006 Zurich Classic of New Orleans! Unlike the putt, however, a chip shot requires you to decisively strike down on the ball, therefore you need to adjust your setup position slightly from that of the putt, to assure that you do so.

You do this in two interrelated ways: First you move the ball back from the (approximate) three-inch position inside of your left heel, where it was when putting, to a point past or behind the middle of your stance line, which automatically positions your hands more forward in relation to the ball. This rearward ball position also automatically creates a club shaft that leans or tilts even more pronouncedly forward now, than it did when you addressed a putt, even though, as with putting, your chip shot address and impact positions are basically the same.

As the chip shot lengthens and the swing gets longer, it will be less critical to have a back-in-the-stance ball position, but more on this in the next chapter, dealing with the pitch shot and Dynamic Number Three, Loading.

To aid us in achieving a forward swing bottom on your chipping strokes, you employ the aiming point technique. Simply put, the aiming point technique refers to how the mind, at the top of the backstroke, actively directs the hands to a point in front of the ball along the ball-to-target line (also called the straight plane line,

Here I am demonstrating the dynamic impact position of chip shots. Note the amount of forward lean of the club shaft. Without the aid of full loading and the use of the pivot, such forward lean (established at address) is needed to get the swing bottom in front of the ball, to create dynamic impact. *(Photo by Kerry Corcoran.)*

which is the Fifth Dynamic). In order to move the bottom of your swing arc and the center of your divot forward of the ball, you have to aim your hands forward of the ball before starting your downswing as this will insure that you strike your chip shot solidly before the club head reaches the low point of the swing.

Look at this photo of me at the completion of my backswing on a chipping stroke (page 39, left). We've drawn a line from my hands to my aiming point in front of the ball, to give you a graphic illustration of just how the concept works. Now look at this photo at the top of my backswing in a full swing (right). You can see how the same aiming point line exists, but as a longer line between the hands and the point in front of the ball. In other words, just as a chip shot represents a longer putting swing, the full swing extends the same basic motion even more.

How far ahead of the ball do you think the low point, or swing bottom, of your chipping stroke lies? You may find it surprising that the answer is four inches, which, as you recall from the survey in the book's introduction, represents its same ideal location on full swing shots. However, the aiming point technique isn't so specific that it requires you to aim your hands precisely to an exact, four-inch point in front of your ball along the plane line. Rather, you simply want to cultivate the mental awareness of directing the hands to a point in front of the ball and not at the ball itself. If you aim your hands directly at the ball, your swing will indeed reach its bottom or low point, either at the ball or, more than likely, behind it. You may get away with the former, but a rearward swing bottom almost always yields disastrous results.

Just as with putting, you want your mind to be "in your hands," because as soon as you think about moving the club head itself, you lose consciousness of your hands' job of keeping your grip pressure even during the chipping stroke. Indeed, thinking of the club head, instead of the hands, results in a flippy swing from the wrists that causes the club head to drop too soon behind the ball or right at the ball.

Bobby uses the aiming point concept whether he is hitting a short chip shot or a full 7-iron shot. In both cases, he constructs an imaginary line between his hands at the end of his backstroke or backswing to a point along his plane line in front of the ball. (In the photo of him hitting the chip shot, the tee indicates his aiming point.) *(Photos by Kerry Corcoran.)*

Therefore, you simply want to aim your hands as far forward of the ball as you need, to create a swing bottom (again as it's measured by the center or deepest spot in the divot) that is four inches forward of the ball. Because different people have different physiques, abilities, different hand speeds, and perhaps different length clubs, and stand at different distances from the ball,

each golfer will have to find his or her own aiming point location, which trial and error will accomplish.

In many ways, the aiming point technique represents a dynamic swing's "unifying principle," as its successful execution does much to insure a flat left wrist and a forward-leaning club shaft at impact, as well as a forward swing bottom. As your swing grows from the putt to the chip, to our next chapter's shot, the pitch, and then on to the full swing, the aiming point technique will also do much to assure that your swing stores its loaded energy with needed lag.

In my rookie year on tour, 1980, I began to establish some great friendships with some of the veterans of the tour, including

If you aim your hands at the ball, or if your mind gets focused on the club head instead of the hands, you will surely become master of the "chili dip," that dreaded, duffed chip that begs us, crying for mercy, caused from a swing bottom being too far behind, or rather, not far enough in front of the ball. Establishing a proper setup position, with the forward lean of the club shaft, is the first step toward a "dip" cure. (Note that in the last picture the divot occurred behind the ball as a result.) *(Photos by Kerry Corcoran.)*

Johnny Miller, Billy Casper, Hubert Green, Andy Bean, Morris Hatalsky, Curtis Strange, Greg Norman, and many others. I would often engage them in little games around the pratice green, much as I did during my teenage years at Carmel Valley Golf and Country Club. These great players never made me, the new kid on the block, feel like I was being too forward; rather, they welcomed this relaxing form of competition and were open and engaging in conversation. In fact, I felt we all learned from each other.

During the Hawaiian Open in 1981, I was practicing short chip shots with Hubert Green, who I think was (and, perhaps, as he now competes on the Champions Tour, still is) the best chipper in the history of the game. Hubert took me to the cleaners that afternoon, but in so doing gave me one of the best chipping tips that I ever received, which was to use a more lofted club than I was using. Instead of using an 8- or 9-iron, Hubert suggested I use a sand wedge, and position the ball farther back in my stance at address, which would automatically move my hands farther ahead of the ball. This would also create an even more pronounced forward lean of the club shaft at address, for a more pronounced downward angle of attack at the ball through the impact zone.

As he explained to me, increasing this angle of descent to the ball allowed for greater consistency in chipping from all kinds of different lies. For example, if the ball were in the rough, such a setup position would allow less grass to get caught between the club face and the ball at impact. This will insure more solid club-face-to-ball contact and more consistent results. Should the ball be sitting down in a hole or in bad lie, Hubert's setup suggestion allowed me to strike the ball higher on the club face, for a more solid hit at impact, and solid contact is a golfer's number-one goal on all shots.

During the early eighties, I was also selected to be on *Golf Magazine*'s "Champs Clinic" panel to answer questions golfers sent in. Even back then, I loved helping people with their golf swings, and I refused to allow the ghost writers to answer the questions for me, with my name attached to it. Looking back, I wish I had the knowledge I have today, for my answers would have been different than they often were.

I remember getting questions like: *Dear Bobby: I hit the ball off a tee pretty well, but when I have to hit off the ground, my shots are much worse. What can I do?* Answer: Get your swing bottom more forward! *Dear Bobby: I'm pretty good with my short irons, but with the longer clubs I have more difficulty. Why's that?* Answer: Get your swing bottom more forward! *Dear Bobby: My golf club has really lush fairways. I play to a twelve handicap, but when I go to my friend's club, where the fairways are cut much shorter, I can't break 100. Can you help?* Answer: Get your swing bottom more forward! *Dear Bobby: My teacher says I scoop the ball too much, and the ball never seems to penetrate the wind. Why's that?* Answer: Get your swing bottom more forward! *Dear Bobby: I hit the ball fat, and I chili-dip chip shots a lot with my club hitting behind the ball and into the ground. Now I'm scared, so I putt the ball instead. Do you have any ideas?* Answer: Get your swing bottom more forward!

The list of questions would go on, and to a vast majority of them I would have offered this same answer.

Keep in mind that even PGA Tour players, the best golfers in the world, can forget to allow their minds to control their hands when chipping. That's when they hit those fat, chili-dipped shots that make them look so much like amateurs out for a Sunday round, rather than the finely tuned and well-trained athletes that they obviously are.

In addition to fat chips, those bladed or thinly sculled shots that send the ball scurrying across the green like a jackrabbit also stem from a rearward, rather than a forward swing bottom. If the fat chip results from the golfer not directing the club sufficiently forward to their aiming point, thin chips happen when the player, fearing that he or she will hit behind the ball into the ground, lifts and swings the club sharply upward through impact, thus catching the ball incorrectly in its middle, rather than at its bottom or base where it rests on the ground.

You use a little bit of body motion, called the pivot, to move the club when chipping. More specifically, you initiate the backstroke of the chip with your shoulders moving your arms and hands, while you move the club on the downstroke of the chip with your hips. This small pivoting action shifts your weight ever so slightly back, then forward through the impact zone, just as the slight turning or pivoting motion of the body that accompanies it transfers speed and motion to the arms and into the club. This gives your swing enough force to strike the ball with a downward accelerating motion, and enough speed to allow your chipping stroke to achieve a forward swing bottom.

This sequencing of the body's pivot, i.e., starting the backswing with your shoulders, and the downswing with your hips, is the same, whether you are hitting a chip, a pitch, or a full shot. This keeps your swing thoughts simple, regardless of the length of swings you are making, and makes it easier to perform all shots under pressure on the course.

I'm amazed that some instructors teach an entirely unique and different chipping stroke than the one they teach for the pitch shot and full swings. Players who learn in this manner are then forced to implement a whole new swing on shots that may be very similar in length. At what point do they switch from their chipping stroke swing into their pitching stroke swing? They obviously will have to pick a precise point in their backswing when they switch gears from chipping to pitching, and this can only add complexity and confusion to the execution of both types of shots.

Therefore, it makes far more sense to learn the fundamentals of the pivot as early on as you are doing here with the chip, because this will enable golfers to easily extend and repeat the pivot on pitch and full swings. In fact, golfers will come to think of this small chipping stroke, employed with a correct and well-controlled pivoting motion, as their loyal friend, one that will all but assure a solid and efficient passage through the impact zone, regardless of the length of their shots.

Just as you used your body for the first time when chipping, the shot also introduces the cocking and uncocking of the left wrist during the back and through swings. This nudges you toward the Number Three and Four Dynamics of loading and lagging the club. Simply put, any time the club approaches hip height as you swing it on the backswing, there is usually an accompanying cocking of the left wrist (some golfers purposely delay their wrist cock until later in the swing), which is a more difficult and sophisticated move requiring great timing.

Here's a simple exercise that teaches the wrist cock, and it's one you can do in your living room with any golf club. Grip a club with your left hand alone (with your right hand if you are a left-handed golfer), and extend your left arm and club so they form a straight line that's horizontal to the ground. Now, cock your left wrist up, and the club with it, by using the muscles of the last three fingers of the left hand. Do not move your arm as you cock your wrist, and stop when the club and your left arm form a right angle, or the letter "L." You have just learned the backswing's left-wrist cock.

Now, lower the club along with the top of your wrist to form a straight and level line—meaning that the club shaft is once again parallel to the ground. This is the flat-left-wrist alignment that we want to achieve at impact with all shots. Finally, relax your left wrist and allow the weight of the club head to drop the club toward the ground, below its straight alignment with the left arm. You have just learned to fully uncock the club.

Remember, however, that because the chipping stroke is small, you will barely cock your wrist on the backstroke. Some golfers opt for an almost completely stiff-wristed style of chipping, but even they want to uncock their left wrists through impact to en-sure a downward blow onto the ball. The good news is that grav-ity helps to do this naturally, if we sufficiently relax our left arms and wrists through the entire chipping motion. As you will see in pitching and swinging, the additional centrifugal force of the longer swings make this uncocking action even more inevitable.

Now, this is good and bad news, because the number-one job, function, and goal of all of our swing dynamics is to prevent this uncocking of the left wrist (and, therefore, the club head) from happening too soon. That is to say, we don't want the club head uncocking behind the ball, but in front of it.

Here's a story about learning to chip that I never tire of repeating. Once more it involves Ben Doyle, my childhood instructor, and it both captures Ben's inimitable teaching style and his unsurpassed knowledge of golf. It seems that Ben was teaching a man the chipping stroke by having this fellow do nothing but hit 10-yard chip shots during the entire course of an hour's lesson. Later that day the student went over to play Spyglass Hill, and, after his round, came back to Ben ecstatic about his play. "I shot seventy-eight," the man proudly proclaimed. "It was the best round of my life!" Ben answered, "That's good, but if you only had hit the chip shot you learned in your lesson earlier in the day on each shot, all the way around the course, you would have shot three hundred, but you would have become so good at it!"

In Ben's student's defense, not many people have enough patience to work on the chipping stroke for the full hour of a lesson; most want to move on to their full swings almost immediately, if not work on them exclusively. To Ben's credit, he didn't really expect this man to chip his way around Spyglass Hill. Rather, he made that comment to emphasize the importance of a flat left wrist at impact, and the role it plays in hitting solid shots of all lengths.

Look at the photographs on page 49 of me hitting a chip shot during the sand drill and see what you can learn from them. Notice how I maintain my flat left wrist through the entire swing, and how it and my forward-leaning club shaft at impact produce the desired downward angle of attack onto the ball necessary for a forward swing bottom. In the first chapter, I pointed out that when the flat left wrist breaks down while putting, the club shaft swings past the hands before it decelerates to try to realign itself with the left wrist and arm. When you decelerate your chipping stroke, the left wrist also collapses and the left arm and club shaft almost come to a stop. All that is left for you to do is to clean up the mess that results from your chili-dipped (or bladed) chips.

CHIPPING DRILLS

The Sand Drill

It's time to have some fun in the sand, and rather than the bunker representing a hazard for you, this time it provides an opportunity for you to work on both your aiming point technique and your forward swing bottom. Just as I described it in the introduction, the sand drill begins by your drawing a straight line in the sand. Next, use your sand wedge and address that line as if it were the ball, and you were preparing to hit a chip shot. Now simply make the chip shot swing that you learned in this chapter. Even though you will not use a ball, I want you to employ the aiming point technique by directing your hands to a point well in front of this line. The goal is for your club to enter the sand at the front edge of this line, then to continue swinging down and forward, so that the center of the divot lies four inches in front of the line, and so that you strike the sand with a flat left wrist. Look at this picture of me executing the sand drill with my wedge, and at my chipping stroke. You may be surprised, but the photos indisputably prove that, even with the small chipping stroke swing, the center of the divot does indeed fall four inches in front of the line.

The Cross-hand Chipping Drill

Get off the couch and take the lead from PGA Tour winner Chris Couch, who won the 2006 Zurich Classic at New Orleans with a dramatic cross-handed chip in on the eighteenth hole. Do so by practicing your chipping with a cross-handed grip. Doing so will help you ingrain the feeling of a solid and flat left wrist at impact on all of your shots. Using the chipping stroke that you learned in this chapter, swing your lower left hand and arm (the right hand if you're a lefty) at the same pace and speed

The goal of the sand drill is to make swings in which the leading edge of the club strikes the sand just in front of the line (indicating the ball position), and continues to swing downward and forward, to the bottom of the swing arc, four inches in front of the line. Here Bobby demonstrates the sand drill with a chipping stroke. *(Photos by Kerry Corcoran.)*

as your entire club (club head, shaft, and grip), and strike down and through your chip with a flat left wrist at impact, and a forward-leaning club shaft. Use the aiming point technique and work on moving the bottom of your swing arc to its ideal four-inch-forward forward swing bottom location. Don't be surprised that if, after some practice time, you find yourself chipping better cross-handed than you do with a conventional grip. If so, follow Chris's lead and use this grip while chipping on the golf course.

BULLET POINTS

- During the chipping stroke, the club moves downward and strikes the ball before it reaches both the ground and the bottom of its arc. It then continues to descend to its low point of four inches in front of the ball, before it swings back up to complete the stroke.

- The aiming point technique refers to how the mind actively directs the hands to a point in front of the ball along the ball-to-target line. In order to move the bottom of your swing arc and the center of your divot forward of the ball, you have to aim your hands forward of the ball during the swing.

- The number-one job, function, and goal of all of your swing dynamics is to prevent the uncocking of the left wrist (and therefore, the club head) from happening too soon. That is to say, you don't want the club head uncocking behind the ball, but in front of it.

- Use a little bit of body motion, called the pivot, to move the club when chipping. More specifically, you initiate the backstroke of the chip with your shoulders moving your arms, hands, and club, while you move them on the downstroke of the chip with your hips.

- The aiming point technique represents a dynamic swing's "unifying principle," as its successful execution does much to insure a flat left wrist and forward-leaning club shaft at impact, and a forward swing bottom, as well.

CHAPTER THREE

THE PITCH SHOT:

Dynamic #3— Loading

Pitching represents the next step in our incremental journey toward a dependably dynamic golf swing and game. To review, chipping added Dynamic Number Two, The Forward Swing Bottom, to Dynamic Number One, The Flat Left Wrist, which we learned in putting.

Dynamic Number Three, Loading, extends this swing's motion from the chip into the pitch shot, which in many ways represents a miniature version of the full swing. Before proceeding, I want golfers to ingrain in their minds the idea that it is a dynamic swinging motion that produces good golf shots, regardless of length, and that nothing disrupts the application of your swing dynamics more than fixing your attention on the golf ball and the golf clubs themselves. Rather, you want your mind to "be in your hands," as my old teacher Ben Doyle used to say to me, because, like an orchestra leader waving his baton, the hands lead the way in producing rhythmic and effectively dynamic golf swings. It is only by remaining consciously aware of your hands throughout your entire swing that you can keep them from instinctively taking over and becoming too active at the wrong time in your motion. What's more, as you learned via the aiming point technique, your hands direct your swing to their proper forward-of-the-ball impact location, and in so doing act as captains that steer the ship of your swing to its predetermined destination.

Specifically, when hitting pitch shots, you want to think about and monitor the cocking of your left wrist, which, when added to the basic chipping motion that you learned in the previous chapter, converts the chipping stroke into a pitching swing. This cocking of the left wrist sets our Number-Three Dynamic, "loading," into action.

"Well, Bobby, that's fine, but what exactly is "loaded" when we make a pitching swing?"

That's a good question. What the wrist cock "loads" is power, and it does so by adding leverage to the golf swing. Think of it this way: In the putting and chipping strokes, the left arm and club shaft remain in a relatively straight line throughout the motion. In other words, these strokes require no, or minimal, wrist cock. Because pitch shots are longer shots, you need more power with which to hit them, and it is the added leverage and free-swinging motion of the club, created by the left wrist cock, that provides this power for you.

The more you load the club via the left wrist cock, the more power you build into your swing. Think of loading one of those old-styled muskets, or winding the rubber-powered propeller of a balsa-wood model airplane. The more the powder is compressed and loaded into the chamber, and the tighter you wind the rubber band propeller, the stronger and more powerful the gunshot, and the faster the plane will fly. Likewise in a golf

Note how the left wrist is nearly fully cocked and loaded before the left arm reaches the first parallel-to-the-ground position during the backstroke. From this position, I simply complete my backstroke to allow the pivot to deliver the loaded club through impact. I make no attempt to manually release or unload the club through impact. Centrifugal force takes care of all the release. *(Photo by Kerry Corcoran.)*

swing, the stronger you load the club in the backswing, by cocking your left wrist, the more powerfully you will be able to hit the ball.

You can also measure the load by the angle between the left wrist and arm and the club shaft, once the left wrist cock has set the club in the backswing. The smaller this angle, the more you

Note the positions of John Daly and Tiger Woods at the top of their backswings. Both have fully loaded their drivers, yet the lengths of their swings vary. John Daly's left wrist cocks and cups, allowing an even fuller load of the club, as opposed to Tiger Woods, who has the more conventional (i.e., a flatter, or at least not as severely cupped top of the backswing) left wrist position. To be a power hitter you can never load the club too much on the backswing, but your downswing dynamics must be able to support the extra power and speed of this load. (More about this in the next chapter.) *(Photos by Warren Keating. Used with the permission of the PGA Tour and CBS Sports.)*

have loaded the club; and this in turn creates more potential energy, via the wider opening of this angle, as centrifugal force straightens it through the impact zone.

Keep in mind, however, that because a pitch swing is shorter than a full swing, you do not have enough time to load the club as strongly as you do when hitting full shots.

Because you load the club the same way, whether pitching or swinging, let's look at some Swing Vision photos of tour players who have loaded their clubs exceptionally well while making full swings.

Many professionals refer to this loading of the club and cocking of the left wrist as the "hinging of the club" on the backswing, and I like the term "hinging" because it makes me think of the hinges on a trunk in which you might store extra blankets. To open that trunk, you would stand directly behind it and pull up

The loading of the club is like a hinge on a trunk that lifts vertically. *(Photo by Kerry Corcoran.)*

its lid. In other words, the top of the trunk swings up on its hinges; and it is this exact vertical motion the left wrist mirrors in loading the club by elevating it up in the air on the backswing. This move, which you will see begins at the very start of a pitch swing, is so vitally important for golfers to play their best, that it never ceases to amaze me how often so many golf instructors fail to emphasize it in their teaching and writing.

While the old Scottish saying, "You don't hit the ball with the backswing," has a kind of *Golf In the Kingdom* ring to it, I disagree, because only when the club is properly loaded on the backswing can we swing it more dynamically on the down-and-through swing. That's because properly loading the club on the backswing gives you the best chance to more easily and repetitively achieve both a flat left wrist and a forward swing bottom through the impact zone.

Round out your understanding of why this is true by taking an inverse look at what happens when golfers fail to load their club efficiently on a pitching stroke backswing. First, when they reach the top of their poorly-loaded swing, golfers feel themselves in a weak position that lacks the power they need to strike their shot solidly into the air. Then, in an unconscious attempt to add power and speed during their downswing, they uncock their left wrist too soon, so that it does not arrive at impact in a flat position. The cupping of the wrist at impact adds extra loft to the club that is not needed, as pitching or sand wedges have plenty of loft built into them already. The breaking down of the left wrist, as you have seen with chipping, also moves the bottom of the swing arc behind the ball, instead of in front of it where our Number-Two Dynamic, the forward swing bottom, tells us it belongs.

Beginning golfers should learn to correctly load a pitch shot with a wedge before they ever take the driver out of the bag, and experienced golfers who are unable to hit full shots with a flat left wrist at impact should back up a step and focus all their attention on learning the proper loading action through the pitching stroke, before moving on. It's never to late to learn and improve, and though it may mean you'll have to give up that five-dollar Nassau round of golf with your buddies for a couple of Saturdays while you work on your dynamics on the range, your game will reap some great dividends by doing so. In fact, I truly hope that I never again hear the lament of the teaching pro about students who grow impatient with learning proper swing dynamics, via the pitch shot, and insist they spend their entire lessons hitting drivers.

Remember to use the same aiming point technique that you

So critical is properly loading the club that I had these photos taken from many different angles, revealing the load on the pitch shot. (*Photos by Kerry Corcoran.*)

learned in the previous chapter on chipping when you deliver the
club to the ball, through the impact zone, on your pitch shots. To
review, the aiming point technique involves picking a spot forward of the ball along the ball-to-target line. At the top of the
pitching swing you aim your hands at the spot, and not at the ball
at all. The aiming point technique does wonders in helping you
move the bottom of your swing arc forward of the ball, in order to
strike down on it with a flat left wrist and a forward-leaning club
shaft.

Look at the tilt of my head and where my eyes appear to be looking. That's right, they are directed at the aiming point, not at the ball. *(Photo by Kerry Corcoran.)*

Now I want to talk about an important though often overlooked trait that the chip and pitch shot swings share, a trait that distinguishes them from the full swing: Both the chipping and pitching strokes end at or just past the follow-through position.

What do I mean by the "follow-through position?" One of the biggest misconceptions about golf technique is that the swing's finish and follow-through positions are one and the same thing. In fact, the swing's follow-through ends at that point or position relatively quickly after impact, when both arms are straight, while the finish of the swing extends well beyond this point, and finds either the left or both elbows bent.

"Well, Bobby," I suspect some of you may be thinking, "You're just splitting hairs about the difference between the follow-through and finish positions!"

I must respectfully disagree, and here's why. . . .

Most golfers facing a pitch shot of about 15 yards often take a nice, smooth backswing, and even load the club reasonably well. Then, because they do not have a clear mental image of the length of their through swing (i.e., they don't understand the difference between the follow-through and the finish positions), they often will slow their swings down as their clubs enter the impact zone, in a misguided attempt not to hit their pitch shots too far.

However, as you've seen, even when putting, any effort to slow down the club through the impact zone leads to the flat left wrist breaking down and the right wrist straightening. Again, as the wrist uncocks prematurely, the golfer will dump the club into the ground behind the ball, rather than creating a swing bottom in front of it. The good news is that, by knowing that your pitch swing ends in the follow-through position, with both arms straight or just past that point in the swing, you can confidently strive to accelerate the club though impact on your pitch shots. Now you can strike down on the ball with a flat left wrist and a forward swing bottom of four inches in front of the ball.

Let's look at these pictures of me pitching the ball and see what they reveal. First, I have a stance slightly wider than I do when chipping, yet it is still as open as it is in the chip stroke. This openness of the stance is really more of a style issue, but I've found that a slightly open stance while pitching does help with the implementation of proper swing dynamics. This is because an open stance opens the hips and gives them the freedom to rotate, which keeps the club on its proper arc, while the hands and wrists sustain the load throughout the downswing. As swing speed increases in the full shots, you no longer benefit from an open stance at address, because the hips during a full swing turn much harder and faster on the downswing.

Next, notice that I have placed the ball near the center of my stance, or forward of its position, for the chip stroke. Notice also that I'm maintaining good address posture, meaning that my back and spine angle aren't slouching. I initiate my backswing by cocking the left wrist and by a quiet and small pivoting motion of the feet, knees, hips, and shoulders (the pivot is a blend of a rearward shifting of weight and a circular turning of the body), so that the left wrist cocks or hinges to the 90-degree point by the time my left arm is parallel, or slightly short of parallel to the ground. I have now completed the backswing loading action, which signals the end of my pitching stroke backswing.

Remember, because the pitch shot requires a relatively small swing, you want to let your hands begin to cock, or hinge, and therefore load the club right from the very moment you begin your motion. I believe that the earlier you can set the club, the more precise and controlled that set and load will be to create all the power you will need through the impact zone.

Pages 62–64: Here Bobby makes a complete pitching stroke. (*Photos by Kerry Corcoran.*)

It bears repeating that this early cocking of the club with the left wrist also greatly facilitates a flat left wrist at impact, as well as a forward swing bottom after impact, because the golfer will feel less inclined to uncock the club prematurely, as the club approaches the ball, in an attempt to add power to the stroke.

Some talented athletes can lag (our next dynamic) so well on the downswing of their full swings that they achieve dynamic impact without fully loading the club on the backswing. I believe that this is a gift. Bill Rogers had it in the seventies and eighties, and was player of the year in 1981. Sergio Garcia and Lucas Glover, to name two contemporary PGA Tour players, have the talent to do it. Some say that I had that ability as well. The key is that whatever it takes to produce dynamic impact, do it! But regardless of the style changes you may make in your swing, never neglect your dynamics while making them. If there is one lesson I have learned in my golf career that I can share with you, this is it: Never, ever, give up your dynamics while pursuing style!

Now back to the task at hand. If the cocking of the left wrist builds power during the backswing, then retaining the angle between the left wrist and the club shaft "stores" that loaded power until impact. The forward pivoting motion of the body initiates the pitch shot's downswing, while the mental focus throughout the downswing is on keeping the left wrist cocked for as long as is

feasible. As I've said, letting one's attention shift to the ball and the club head is a great disrupter of sustained dynamics through the impact zone. Even if the golfer has hinged his or her wrists and the club fully on the backswing, normal human anxiety can easily take over, and an overeagerness to hit at the ball, rather than swing through it, can convulsively flip the club head prematurely, meaning prior to impact. The great Ben Hogan said that "Impact should be incidental to the swing," meaning that the ball should never be the focus of the swing, it should just get in its way through the impact zone.

The key to understanding how to do this is realizing that the left wrist will uncock before impact completely on its own during the downswing, as a result of combined centrifugal force and gravity. In fact, there isn't a human being on earth that can stop it from doing so. I can't say the following more emphatically: *Any uncocking or unhinging of the wrists during the early stages of the downswing, in an attempt to add power, speed, and/or loft to the club, greatly decreases the chance you have of striking the ball with a flat left wrist and a forward swing bottom through the impact zone.*

Recently, I was at the TaylorMade factory in Carlsbad, California, testing drivers, and thought it is kind of freaky how technologically advanced the game has become. For example, it really isn't

necessary to watch the flight of the ball anymore, since club fitters and testers use computerized launch monitors to give you your impact and flight data information. Every golfer wants to increase his or her ball speed (which equates to added distance), myself included; so, with the help of the launch monitor, I put some of my swing knowledge to the test. My normal swing with a driver produced around 160 mph of ball speed. When I would really swing hard, I could get up into the mid-160s. Then I thought about maximizing the load and sustaining it as long as possible on the downswing. I amazed the technicians when I announced, "Watch this!" Voila, my swing speed hit 170+ mph, and the ball went straight.

How important to me is the loading of the club in the backswing? It has been the number-one thing I have focused on and strived to perfect throughout most of my career. In fact, I was caught a bit unaware when my writing partner, Andy Brumer, told me that none other than the great Bobby Jones said in his instruction film that cocking his left wrist was the one fundamental that he worked the hardest on to successfully accomplish; so, evidently, there is an illusive element to Dynamic Number Three, which should motivate all of us to continue to work on it.

In fact, no teacher of mine really ever focused on the dynamic of loading the club, except for Ben Doyle. He didn't care when I loaded, just that I did. He never tried to change my natural propensity to load late. But, in 1981 I made a significant swing change, in that I began to load the club sooner on my backswing. I felt this earlier load helped create a smoother transition from backswing to downswing and made my swing less timing-dependent. I still had to focus on completing the load at the top of the backswing, but the load was more complete near the top, so less effort was necessary to fully load the club. Any move that simplifies the swing is profitable. After making the change, which improved my dynamics, I made eleven cuts in a row and had several top-ten finishes, including three in second place.

Because the pitching stroke is considerably longer than the

chip shot, you need to add a bit more body pivot, both back and through the ball. Therefore, it is not essential to address a pitch shot with your hands and club shaft leaning forward, as you did when chipping. You may do so if you want to, but, again, this is a matter of style.

I recommend that you address your pitch shots with your hands centered along your body, so that the butt end of the club points directly to your belt buckle. Now, this address position makes it easier to shift your weight slightly to your right or rear foot, as you begin your small but essential pivoting motion.

Note that when Bobby sets up for a 7-iron shot, his hands and club shaft are in the same centered position as they are when he plays a pitch shot. *(Photo by Kerry Corcoran.)*

Extending your chipping stroke into a pitch shot swing requires you to turn your shoulders a little bit more, as well. This creates a little more swinging motion of the arms, whose momentum, in turn, helps to smoothly cock the club upward into its loaded state. Keeping the grip pressure nice and light, while still maintaining full control of the club, facilitates and blends together this swinging/setting/loading action. Addressing the pitch (and the full swing) with the club centered in relation to your body at address, rather than leaning it forward, also facilitates the cocking of the left wrist and, hence, the loading of the club.

Golfers certainly do have the style option of addressing the pitch (and the full swing) shot with a flat-left-wrist impact alignment. However, even when choosing to do so, address and impact on these shots are dynamically different, because the loading of the club, and successfully storing that load, automatically moves the swing bottom forward. That means that while the left wrist is still flat at impact, the club will lean even more forward of its address position when pitching and swinging.

This is why my writing partner, Andy Brumer, likes to talk about this book as having an "optimistic," as in a "forward"-looking, swing philosophy and message.

In fact, from your visual perspective when hitting the shot (i.e., what your two eyes literally see as you swing), your flat left wrist will now appear to almost cover your left foot at impact. If you start with the hands in a body-centered position, they will really travel quite a distance on the way to reaching their impact destination.

It's not just your hands that move forward through the impact zone. Indeed, your whole body also shifts forward of its address position through the impact zone. Only your head remains relatively steady and positioned where it was at address, until the momentum of the swing allows it to rise after impact.

Now I'd like to invite you back into the sand bunker, where you will take your wedge and draw a line in the sand representing

You can really see the difference here between Corey Pavin's address and impact positions with his driver. At address, his hands and club shaft are positioned in the center of his body; at impact, his hands are well forward and his club shaft leans pronouncedly forward. *(Photos by Warren Keating. Used with the permission of the PGA Tour and CBS Sports.)*

your golf ball, just as you did while using this sand drill on your chip shot. I often utilize this drill myself, especially when I am not pleased with how I am striking my pitch shots; but it is imperative to use this drill when first learning the basic pitching technique. Without it, you will struggle in understanding how to make a proper divot and how to solidly strike the ball.

This time I want you to make your basic pitch shot swing and, using the aiming point technique, direct your hands forward of the line, in order to remove some sand from the bunker. Remembering dynamics number two and three, you want the divot to start right at the line, with its center four inches in front of the ball, after striking the sand with a flat left wrist. Experiment both with moving your aiming point forward and back, and/or the position of the line forward or back in your stance, until you can consistently make a quality divot forward of the line with your pitch stroke.

While you have come to associate pitch shots as those hit with either your pitching, sand, or lob wedges, you can actually

The sand divot's deepest print is four inches in front of the ball. Whether using a ball or not while performing the sand drill, focus on taking the right divot. *(Photo by Kerry Corcoran.)*

execute the pitch shot swing with any club in the bag. In fact, the classic punch shot swing also ends at or just past the both-arms-straight follow-through position, though the punch shot usually employs a slightly longer backswing.

It has become part of the modern game's lore, how a young Spanish boy from a family of modest means, a kid named Seve Ballesteros, used to sneak onto the golf course with a couple of golf balls and the only club he owned, a 3-iron. With that one club, he developed, arguably, greater short game skills and imagination than anyone who has ever played the game. Those formative years remained close to Seve's heart throughout his hall of fame professional career and he often spoke emotionally of them.

I vividly recall how many of us tour players would gather around Seve near the chipping green and driving range bunker during the practice days of our tournaments. We'd watch in awe bordering on disbelief, as he demonstrated hitting high, soft-landing pitch shots, and full sand-explosion shots with his 3-iron.

While I was in college, playing on the golf team for Brigham Young University and our coach, Karl Tucker, we would sometimes change our practice routine and play nine holes using only four clubs. Amazingly, our scores were only a stroke or two worse per nine holes than when playing with a full bag. Learning to improvise and hit a variety of shots is very healthy and helps us to better understand how loading the club relates to a forward swing bottom, and I recommend you doing so at your course, for a relaxing afternoon of nine holes, when the course isn't crowded.

I also competed a couple of times in the World One-Club Championship held near my home, at the Lochmere Golf Club in Cary, North Carolina, where competitors played with a single club, which really forces you to become a shot-maker. There's no doubt that some of this shot-making art has been lost on the PGA Tour, with today's technology and "grip it and rip it" mentality. Certainly, when the tour comes to courses like Pebble Beach, Riviera, and Hilton Head, shaping shots like a true shot-maker becomes more important once again. It isn't surprising that these courses are among the players' favorites, perhaps for that reason.

Pitching the ball well is part of the art of shot-making. Not surprisingly, Tiger Woods and Phil Mickelson, today's number-one and number-two players respectively, are both great pitchers of the ball as well.

As a kid, people often found me with a sand wedge in my hand. It was my favorite club; and though I'm not sure I consciously knew it at the time, the main reason I attached myself so faithfully to it was because the pitching swings I made with it helped me build solid dynamics with *all* of the clubs in my bag. Whether I was in between bites of lunch, in a casual conversation, waiting around the club, or waiting for my mom to pick me up, I often had a sand wedge in my hands and would be practicing my pitch stroke. I'm sure my mom can remember more instances than she would prefer of those times when I had my sand wedge in one hand and the sandwich she made for me in the other!

The sand wedge was also the club I most often used to pitch golf balls from the edge of the driving range into its middle, a bit of improvised practice I began doing when I got my first job, at the Carmel Valley Golf and Country Club picking up the balls from the range, at the age of ten. I still have my first sand wedge, an old Ben Hogan Special. I only used it for three years, but the grooves are so worn that its face is smooth. Though I was just a kid hired to pick the range, that point in my life was where I retired from work and started playing golf "for a living." I may soon have the world's record for the longest retirement. How blessed I've been!

I'd like to tell you a couple of stories that emphasize the essential relationship between loading and shot-making. After all, one of this book's central themes is that the correct production and application of each swing dynamic works to improve all of our shots, from the putt to the drive. The first story involves the great Gary Player, one of the finest shot-makers the game has ever seen.

Gary was playing a practice round at the British Open one year, and as he faced a 150-yard shot, the caddie he was using that week automatically handed Gary his 7-iron. "What are you doing?" Gary sternly asked the caddie. "Well, it's a one-hundred-and-fifty-yard shot, and that's the distance for your seven-iron," the man answered, surprised by the question. If the question surprised this caddie, Gary's actions (the Black Knight certainly knows how to make the most of a dramatic moment when he encounters one) must have truly startled him.

"Drop eight golf balls right on the ground here," he commanded, before proceeding to hit each one of the balls onto the green with his 2- through 9-irons consecutively. "Now, don't assume just because I'm a certain yardage from the cup that I'll use one club to do the job," he reprimanded his caddie. "It's all about *how* you hit the shot, not what club you use!" Setting the club beautifully, as Gary does, has always allowed him to control his shots and play the game creatively.

I had a similar experience to Gary's with a caddie of my own, though, unlike in Gary's practice round, my story unfolded during actual competition. I was eighteen, and I was playing in my first California State amateur tournament. In the semifinal match, I was faced with an into-the-breeze, 135-yard second shot to the par-4 eleventh hole at Pebble Beach. My caddie automatically handed me an 8-iron. I took the club, dropped it back into the bag, and took out the 4-iron, which, if I read his facial expression correctly, convinced my caddie that I had gone completely crazy. I was loading the club great that week, and I felt in full control of my golf swing, which allowed me to hit the prettiest little cut shot into the green, to about eight feet from the cup . . . with a 4-iron from 135 yards!

Again, loading the club well opens up a wealth of shot-making possibilities, and being able to hit a variety of shots allows you to navigate a range of course and weather conditions that just hitting each club one set distance simply cannot deliver. Needless to say, this makes playing golf a lot more fun. In fact, I venture to say that if Mark Twain had loaded his club better, he would have experienced golf not as "a good walk spoiled," but one considerably more enjoyable and spiced up.

Loading the club well, using all the essential dynamics, once helped me cook up a serving of healthy gamesmanship in another tournament. During the 1978 U.S. Amateur, held at the Plainfield Country Club in New Jersey (and won that year by soon-to-be PGA Tour star John Cook), I was competing in a round of match play, when my fellow competitor began eyeing me like a hawk. He looked into my bag to see what club I was using whenever possible. I had had enough of his gamesmanship, so I decided to play a little of my own. On the second par-3, I had the honor, being one up. The shot called for a full 6-iron, but I decided to hit a cut 4-iron, as the hole was slightly downhill. I hit the ball fifteen feet from the hole. He proceeded to respond on cue, and when his 4-iron sailed over the green and under a tree, he looked at me with astonishment. I gave him my best poker face and moved on.

Mind you, this is a common practice, even on the PGA Tour today, but most players have developed the talent to do it inconspicuously. There's not much talent involved, really; it's just a matter of sticking your hand into the cookie jar when Mom or Dad isn't looking. This chap, on the other hand, must have had very permissive parents, because he peered into my golf bag to discern the clubs I was hitting as if he were sitting in front of the TV, riveted to his favorite sitcom!

Had I not worked so hard on learning to load the club well, it could have been me desperately searching for any clue that might have helped me make better shots, instead of being in control of my swing and ball flight and, therefore, capable of hitting a range of shots with any club in the bag.

Now, who are some of the great loaders of the golf club, both on tour today and from eras past? They include Phil Mickelson, Sergio Garcia, Tiger Woods, Jim Furyk, Vijay Singh, Lee Trevino, Bryon Nelson, and Ben Hogan. It just so happens that these players are also some of the game's best pitchers of the ball, and, less surprising, among golf's most elite competitors. Others whose loading action I'd like you to observe on TV or, even better yet, in person when the tour comes to town—but who haven't achieved as much stardom—include Joey Sindelar, Rory Sabatini, Chad Campbell, and Rod Pampling. I also think Johnny Miller, of course a superstar, cocked and loaded the club, then sustained that load through the impact zone, as well as anyone in the history of the game, especially with his iron shots.

If this sounds more like full swing instruction than a pitching lesson, I want to congratulate you, because no dynamic is more important to making repeatedly sound and powerful full swings than the strong and proper loading of power during the backstroke.

The point is that you should, by now, be more familiar and comfortable with how each of your swing dynamics interact with and influence each of the other dynamics. Indeed, I'm asking you to become even more mindful of this as the chapters progress.

DYNAMIC PITCHING AND LOADING DRILLS

1. THE PILLOW PITCH DRILL

Mothers, or roommates may not like the drill I'm about to recommend, because it's one you can do right in the living room. Take a fairway wood, or hybrid club, and find a large pillow and place it on the carpeted floor. Address the pillow as if it were the ball, then make the pitching stroke whose dynamic fundamentals you just learned in this chapter. Allow the resistance that the pillow creates at impact to ingrain the feeling of a flat left wrist at impact and follow-through that we want on the pitch and on all other swings. Notice how far the pillow travels when the stroke is done correctly, as opposed to a pitching stroke when you uncock your left wrist prematurely, causing club head throwaway and a bent left wrist at impact and into the follow-through. Pay attention to the relationship between loading the club well in the backswing and contacting the pillow with a flat left wrist. You can even do this drill while watching one of our televised golf telecasts. But one word of caution, leave the beer in the other room and keep flying pillows away from windows. Flying pillows and beer don't mix! Just ask David Feherty. I think he'll agree!

2. THE GOLF BALL SURROGATE PITCH

When I was going to Robert Louis Stevenson High School, located right off the seventeenth green at Spyglass Hill, on the Monterey Peninsula, I would often take my books and study in those lovely, light-dappled woods. Well, in addition to books, I'd also take my sand wedge, in order to execute the pitching drill of hitting pinecones with a pitching swing. As I've said, it is often an overfocus on the ball and the club head that causes us to release the club too soon, which results in a broken and bent, rather than a flat left wrist at impact, and a rearward instead of a forward swing bottom. If you have no pinecones at your disposal, you can hit tennis balls, plastic whiffle balls, pieces of paper on the ground, cigarette butts, anything that represents a target, other than a golf ball. You'll be amazed at how removing the ball from your gaze and consciousness reestablishes your mental attention back into your hands where it belongs, in order to load and save the power of your swing as long as possible before impact.

3. The Distance-Control Pitching Drill

Because golfers will have to pitch the ball different distances during a round of golf, they must learn to do so without losing their swings' dynamics. This drill simply consists of hitting pitch shots to targets set at 20, 30, 40, and 50 yards away, while paying attention to cleanly executing the triad of dynamics covered to this point in the book (flat left wrist at impact, forward swing bottom, loading) with each swing. Phil Mickelson does this drill regularly, both during his home practice sessions and when he is preparing for a tournament round on the PGA Tour.

BULLET POINTS

- The dynamic of loading, which you achieve by cocking your left wrist, extends this swing's motion from the chip into the pitch shot, which in many ways represents a miniature version of the full swing.

- It is only by remaining consciously aware of your hands throughout your entire swing that you can keep them from instinctively taking over and becoming too active at the wrong time in your motion.

- Beginning golfers should learn to correctly load a pitch shot with a wedge before they ever take the driver out of the bag, and experienced golfers who are unable to hit full shots with a flat left wrist at impact should back up a step and focus all their attention on learning the proper loading action, through the pitching stroke, before moving on.

- The forward-pivoting motion of the body initiates the pitch shot's downswing, while the mental focus throughout the downswing is on keeping the left wrist cocked for as long as feasible. Letting your attention shift to the ball and the club head is another great disrupter of sustained dynamics through the impact zone.

- Who are some of the great "loaders" of the golf club, both on tour today and from eras past? They include Phil Mickelson, Sergio Garcia, Tiger Woods, Jim Furyk, Vijay Singh, Lee Trevino, Bryon Nelson, and Ben Hogan. It just so happens that these players are also some of the game's best pitchers of the ball and, less surprising, among golf's most elite competitors.

CHAPTER FOUR

THE FULL SWING:

Dynamic #4—
Lag and the Body Pivot
(The Golf Swing's Workhorse)

Now that you have learned to make a dynamic pitch shot swing, it's time to max out the length of your motion into an actual full golf swing. Doing so involves storing the power that you established, set, and loaded in the club via Dynamic Number Three, and retaining this power until we deliver it to the ball through the impact zone. This is the job of Dynamic Number Four, which we call "Lag." How important is lag to golfers' efforts to play their best games? Well, Homer Kelley, in *The Golfing Machine,* anointed lag as "the secret of golf." That about says it all.

However, before you delve into lag itself, you must first learn how to extend your swing from the pitching stroke into a full swing motion, because it is not until you reach the completion of your backswing that you establish lag to store your loaded power.

Note the club is fully loaded as it nears the top of the backswing, then lag begins during the transition into the downswing, increasing the angle of the club shaft to the left arm. *(Photos by Kerry Corcoran.)*

In other words, lag not only belongs to the downswing part of your motion, *it is the downswing's number-one priority, concern, and goal,* until you've swung well past the both-arms-straight, follow-through position. That's when momentum takes you to the finish of your swing.

In conjunction with learning how to establish lag, you need to work on refining your body's work, meaning your pivot motion. If the power that you lag into impact is your precious cargo, the pivot is the transportation vehicle that carries the goods through the impact zone. That is why we call the pivot the golf swing's workhorse.

First off, because a full swing generates more club head speed and hits the ball farther than a pitch shot, you need a stronger foundation or setup position for your swing. This means you want to take a wider stance than you did while chipping or pitching, with your feet spread to shoulder width. You want to make sure you have good posture, with an erect spine that nevertheless tilts at the waist, and knees that bend slightly, with your weight evenly distributed between both feet.

I've also recommended that you make sure you address the ball with the club in a centered position, with the top of the grip pointing at your belt buckle, as you did when pitching, as opposed to it leaning forward in a preset impact position, as in the chipping and putting setup. Again, this centered position of the club at address will make it easier to shift your weight back and through when executing your pivot of the full swing.

As I said in the pitching chapter, when you address your shot this way, your left wrist automatically assumes a bent or cupped position, not the flat alignment it had when you were addressing putts and chips. Tiger Woods, Vijay Singh, Mark Calcavecchia, Chad Campbell, and many other players, display this exact bent left wrist, belt-buckle-centered shaft address alignment.

Again I want to point out that this location of the club shaft at address is a style decision. While many golfers prefer this centered position for a full swing, others, such as Jack Nicklaus, forward-press their hands into that preset, forward-shaft-leaning address/impact position, complete with a flat left wrist. However, Jack, during his prime, had a tremendously skilled and aggressive weight shift in both directions, so he hardly needed any of the help a centered club position at address would have given him in transferring his weight throughout his swing. Having said that, Tiger Woods, who has as good a weight shift as anyone in

Note the centered club-shaft alignment of Tiger Woods and Vijay Singh. *(Photos by Warren Keating. Used with the permission of the PGA Tour and CBS Sports.)*

the game today (and maybe ever), addresses his full shots with his hands more centered than forward.

Though one can create good swing dynamics with either a forward-press address or a centered-club-shaft address, my personal style preference, and what, again, I'm recommending for you, is the latter option, not only because it facilitates the weight shift, as mentioned, but for other reasons as well. One is that, in this position at address, the club will stand at its natural lie angle on the ground, meaning almost straight up and down, and not leaning forward. This helps you to line up correctly, because the almost-vertical club shaft creates an easy, right-angle reference marker in relation to the target. Another is that the cupped left wrist allows for a stronger cocking and loading action during the backswing. As I said repeatedly in the previous chapter, a stronger load results in more power through the impact zone.

Many will argue that the benefit of the slightly bent left wrist also produces a more open club face at the top of the backswing. Again, club face position at the top is another style element, it is not a dynamic of the swing itself. Too many teachers have placed excessive focus on club-face angles at the top of the swing (i.e., is it closed, open, or square?), but this should really be placed down near the bottom of any list of swing priorities. If the club face's position at the top is really so important, why was Tiger Woods able to win the Masters in 1997 by twelve strokes with a closed club-face position, only to change it and win his subsequent majors with a more open one?

Many great golfers have played from a shut-face position at the top, such as Lee Trevino, Paul Azinger, Bernhard Langer, Arnold Palmer, Nancy Lopez, and many others. In other words, the club face's position at the top has little to do with its movement through the impact zone, and it's time the entire teaching establishment turns away from style and more squarely toward dynamics.

Because the full swing displays the longest arc, requires the most body motion, and generates more club head speed than do the shorter swings, it is imperative that you execute it with good, solid posture. We can draw an analogy between the body supporting the golf swing and a work of great engineering, such as the Golden Gate Bridge in San Francisco: Both need to be structurally sound and strong enough to support their respective loads. We might also say that, just as the grapes that produce fine wine need great soil from which to grow, your swing needs a solid setup foundation as well, in order for your dynamics to spring into action.

Tiger works incessantly and methodically on his posture, as do most of the players on tour today. In fact, the importance of good posture has become such an avowed fundamental on tour, that it really isn't that surprising that many of the game's top players address the ball in a relatively similar manner. I might even go as far as to say that, whereas, in the past, posture did often reflect a player's unique style, today, most of the world's elite players look very much alike standing over the ball. This means that, through trial and error, the best golfers in the world have discovered some of the common stylistic elements of good address posture that work to create better swing dynamics. It's no wonder this dynamic posture has to a large degree become customized among tour players.

Let's take a more in-depth look at the setup position for a full swing and talk about how different parts of the body contribute to a great swing pivot, because what ultimately matters is how good posture and the pivot promote, support, and sustain your swing's lag. First of all, at address, you need to have your feet sufficiently wide apart to absorb your weight, as it shifts to the back foot on the backswing, then to the front foot on the forward swing. Many golfers find that a shoulder-width apart serves as a good measurement point. An effectively wide stance like this also facilitates the essential element of good balance throughout the swing, and any sport that involves hitting a ball requires its players to have good balance, so they can apply force to the ball efficiently and effectively.

The pivot blends both lateral and rotational movement, and I believe it is easier to shift laterally, on the balls of the feet, and turn effectively on one's heels. Therefore, I advocate that you set up with your weight evenly distributed to each foot, as this will let you take advantage of the athleticism of the balls of the feet, for good lateral motion, and of the heels, for the purpose of rotation.

Though I may get some nasty letters for this, especially from those who got so angry with Phil Mickelson because of his skiing accident years ago, and with Chris DiMarco more recently, I have found snow skiing to be a great benefit to me in creating greater balance in my golf swing. And, as a quick rebuttal to those nasty letters I'm going to get, let me say: "Quit picking on skiing as a hazardous activity for golfers." Chris DiMarco wrenched his back a year earlier also watching TV at the Masters, Mike Weir (also in 2005) wrenched his back and neck when a stomach virus made him so sick he fell asleep in a bathroom, and Loren Roberts once cracked two ribs by simply coughing, and was off the tour for nearly three months.

The risk of injury while skiing has influenced some tour players, not surprisingly, Phil Mickelson (after his accident) among them, to turn to the balance-enhancing benefits of the martial arts. Some golfers—pros and amateurs alike—practice yoga to improve their game, as they find that this activity, seasoned with centuries of wisdom, balances both the body and the mind. The point to remember is that good balance starts with a firm stance, good posture, and, as in yoga, a clear mental image of the body in a balanced position—and that working on improving your balance in any way you choose will improve your swing's foundation, as well as upgrade its dynamics and consistency.

Next, your knees provide the flexibility you need to make a good pivoting, turning motion. Therefore, you should address the ball with enough knee-bend, so that you feel ready to make a small springing motion, and so that you feel that your body is unlocked and free to move, both in a lateral and rotational manner.

How the two knees bend or don't bend through the swing is, again, a matter of style. It has been popular recently to teach that the right, or back, knee remains bent throughout the entire swing, but many of the best ball-strikers straighten that leg at the completion of the backswing. If *how* the knees bend is a matter of style, the fact that they provide flexibility to the swing is what matters in terms of dynamics.

Let your posterior protrude back a bit at address, as this creates a kind of ballast that provides balance during the swing.

Moving up, anatomically speaking, we arrive at the critical and intricately interrelated elements of the spine and the waist tilt. The spine must remain erect as it tilts the entire upper body from the waist joint forward. How much a golfer tilts is to some extent determined by a golfer's height and the length of the club he or she is hitting; and there is still some degree of style involved in this as well. Again, it's unusual today to see someone stand ramrod erect, as did Mr. Hogan, or slump over the ball, as does the great Japanese player Isao Aoki. The vast majority of top players today have been taught to tilt at about 20 degrees from the hips while hitting a driver, and marginally more as the clubs become shorter through the bag.

In addition to providing structure for the upper body as it pivots, a consistently maintained spine and waist tilt also helps keeps the club swinging on a consistent plane. This is because the shoulders will naturally rotate at right angles to the spine during the swing; and when the shoulders swing on a consistent arc, they keep the club swinging on a steady, unwavering circular plane as well.

There's one stop left up this elevator ride, and that is the head. People probably have heard "keep your head steady" so many

times it makes them sick. What they don't often hear is that a steady head is more the result of a good body pivot than it is an independent swing fundamental in itself. Another way to look at this is to say that, more often than not, golfers' heads become unsteady and sway and bob around too much during the swing *because of their faulty pivots.* But the fact remains that the movement of the head is more of a style issue, though it can affect swing dynamics. Many great players have swayed and/or bobbed their heads during the swing and were still able to employ great dynamics.

Now—about the question of power in the golf swing: How does the pivot create power for you? To answer this important question, let me use the analogy of throwing a baseball, because the golf swing resembles a throwing action as well as the more obvious one of hitting.

If I were to ask you to take a baseball and throw it overhand to someone standing five feet away from you, you would simply take a little step toward that person, and with a small arm move-

Pages 83–85: Note that the great players—like Tiger Woods—have slightly varied styles of knee bend, but they all have some bend in their knees to provide the flexibility to make a good pivoting/turning motion with balance. *(Photos by Warren Keating. Used with the permission of the PGA Tour and CBS Sports.)*

ment, toss him or her the ball, right? Now, if I ask you to imagine you are standing on the pitching mound, trying to throw a one-hundred-mile-an-hour fastball past Alex Rodriguez, you would wind up, shift your weight fully to your back foot, turn your shoulders and hips completely, make a fully long arm motion, take a huge stride forward with your front foot, and fire the ball with all of your body's weight supporting the throw.

These same generalities apply to how you use the body to its fullest during full golf swings, i.e., the longer and harder you want to hit the ball, the larger and fuller you will pivot *instinctively,* without having to think about it.

I'll talk more about the body pivot shortly, but now that you've warmed up your transportation vehicle's engine, its time to turn your attention to just what the pivot delivers through the impact zone, and that is Dynamic Number Four: lag.

From a purely descriptive point of view, "lag" describes the condition of the club head continually trailing the body, arms, and hands—and, of course, the club shaft—right up to impact and through the impact zone, where you want to apply all of your swing's power and energy into the ball. That's a moving, or "kinesthetic," description of what lag looks like.

We can also measure lag, and both further define and, indeed,

Good posture at address helps David Toms utilize his pivot effectively to turn on a consistent arc, which keeps his club well on-plane. *(Photos by Warren Keating. Used with the permission of the PGA Tour and CBS Sports.)*

see it as the size of the angle created between the left arm, wrist, and hand, and the club shaft. The narrower that angle, the more lag you will have at any given measuring point during the down-swing motion.

Lag also involves the stress or bend you place on the club shaft at the start of the downswing. This change of direction, from the top of the backswing to the start of the downswing, adds more load into the club than you created with your wrist cock during the backswing. In other words, very shortly after you start down toward the impact zone, you have stored more loaded power in your club than you had when you reached the top of your swing.

When you successfully create lag in your downswing, you really feel that club head trailing the hands and retaining its stress, or load, in the club shaft. So, lag is both the *quality* of the club head trailing and the *quantity* of the angle between the left arm and the club shaft, *and* the amount of stress or bend you create in that shaft. Remember, lag's job is to store the swing's power right through the impact zone.

Actually, one of the criticisms of my swing people often made when I first came on tour was that it had too much lag. A writer asked my teacher Ben Doyle whether he thought this was true, and if indeed a swing can have too much lag? Ben, with his inimitable wit and insight answered, "Can you have too much love?"— meaning that you can't have too much of a good thing!

The sad truth is that I did begin to lose some of that lag, along with my ability to strike solid golf shots consistently, as my focus shifted to swing style and away from swing dynamics. Mine is truly a cautionary tale, then (which is why I'm repeating it so many times!), as I believe almost every golfer, whose focus turns to making style changes in his or her swing, assumes the very real risk of losing some swing dynamics in the process. Now, I'm not saying that one should never make a style change, but I am saying that one should never lose their focus in creating load and lag in the swing. Tiger has often made style changes, but he never lost the focus on his dynamics. It is possible to play well through swing changes, but only if the dynamics stay in focus.

You took the first step in creating lag in the chipping chapter, when you learned how to set and load the club by cocking your left wrist. We even mentioned that the chipping and the longer putting strokes very often display the beginnings of a wrist cock, and therefore some load and lag as well. It will be your goal in this

full-swing chapter to learn how to sustain and store that load, then to deliver it, via lag, to the ball and through the impact zone. Remember, the longer the club and the faster the swing (they go hand in hand), the more difficult it is to sustain the lag through the impact interval. But stay tuned! We'll show you how it's done!

There is a distinction between lag as a quality, and lag as a quantity. While your goal may be to develop your dynamics to their fullest—meaning, to create as much lag in your downswings as you are individually capable of creating, *the number-one goal that you must achieve now and not later is to create, sustain, and maintain your lag through the impact zone.* The swings of players such as David Toms and Fred Funk, for example, do not exhibit as much of a lag angle as those of Sergio Garcia, Lucas Glover, or Phil Mickelson, halfway into the downswing, but they certainly strike the ball through the impact zone with virtually all of the lag fully intact.

Now, would David and Fred benefit from increasing their lag angles? I think they'd both hit the ball farther if they did, so it's up to them; but they're doing darn well with the swings they presently have, and that's because they've sustained their lag

While David Toms's and Phil Mickelson's lag angles are different halfway through their downswings (Phil's angle is greater), both players sustain the lag right through impact.
(Photos by Warren Keating. Used with the permission of the PGA Tour and CBS Sports.)

through impact. Therefore, allow your lag angle to increase and become stronger, gradually if necessary, as you improve your load and pivot, but, from this moment on, *strive to sustain your lag through the impact zone with every club in your bag and on every swing you make, regardless of the size of your lag angle.*

Now that you've learned the mechanics of creating lag, i.e., a solid stance, and fully cocking the left wrist during the backswing, supported by a balanced pivoting motion, I want to discuss the feel of lag during your downswing.

First off, golfers are often unconscious of the fact that lag is responsible for that coveted feeling of effortless power, when their swings feel free and smooth, their solidly struck shots fly long and straight, and they have the sensation of really accelerating the club into the ball. That's because, when you successfully create lag, you are able to store your power until the last moment, before releasing it through the impact zone.

In other words, the act of efficient storage conserves your energy, so you no longer struggle and strain while swinging. In fact, that awful, awkward, and annoying sensation of gritting your teeth, tensing your muscles, and putting everything you have into hitting the ball—as if you were crouching down to lift a refrigerator—is the sure sign that you have spent your energy well before you even reach the gate of the impact zone, rather than lagging it there. As ironic as this sounds, it actually takes more energy to throw lag away and lose it than it does to sustain it.

Let me recreate the scenario I have encountered over and over again while playing golf with amateurs, whether during pro-ams, corporate outings, or just with my buddies, during a weekend round. A guy will be struggling with his game for a number of holes before he musters up the courage to ask me, "Bobby, what am I doing wrong?" Generally, the better I know the man or woman, the fewer holes it takes for the question to arise (but not always).

"You're swinging too hard," I often tell them, "and therefore you are overaccelerating into the ball."

The main reason people swing too hard, and throw their lag away as if it were a worthless scrap of paper wrapping an energy bar (rather than the energy of the golf swing itself), is that, in their anxious effort to hit the ball so hard, they become overly fixated on the ball. Such ball fixation leads to a premature uncocking of the wrists. This club head throwaway, again, dumps the club behind the ball, instead of driving its forward swing bottom four to five inches in front of the ball.

While you lag the club while chipping and pitching, not only are you trying to create, store, and sustain lag in your full swings, but you now also want to *increase* your swing's lag. In other words, the length of the full swing gives you a greater opportunity to increase your lag on the downswing, and utilize it through the impact zone; and the more you can increase lag, the less chance you will have of throwing it away.

I often get asked during my clinics, after convincing my audience of the need to load and lag the club, "Bobby, just how do I increase lag?" It helps tremendously to exercise the art of visualization, because increasing lag on the downswing is only possible when one has a clear mental image of having fully loaded the club on the backswing, and delaying the release of this load on the downswing.

We spoke of the pivot as the workhorse of your swing, and you've already completed some of the work you needed to help complete your backswing. But the job is only half done, as now you need the pivoting motion of the downswing to relieve your wrists and hands of any tendency they may have to become too active. Only when the wrists remain soft and quiet on the club can your left wrist cock increase your lag, an increase that goes all the way through the impact zone.

Do you remember, in the chipping chapter I said that the hips initiate the shot's downswing? Since you're building your swing incrementally, from the short shots to the long ones, it stands to reason that the hips will work even more authoritatively in the full swing to move your body and club through the impact zone. Indeed, *the number-one key that sustains your lag, from the top of your full swing all the way through the impact zone, is a sound downswing pivot driven and led by the hips, with the shoulders, arms, and, finally, the club trailing throughout the motion.* I said that lag describes the condition of the club *trailing,* and that means something has to be *leading.* What leads are your hips.

Here's a story that really drives home the important role of the pivot-driven hips, as well as the torso and shoulders, in creating lag. It was 1979, and I was playing as a marker in the U.S. Open at Inverness. A marker is a non-competing golfer who forms a twosome with an officially competing golfer during a tournament round, when that golfer's actual playing partner either withdraws or is disqualified from the event. Rather than have the competitor play alone, the USGA, in the case of the U.S. Open, will look for a skilled golfer to join him or her, which keeps the pace of play more uniform and consistent for the rest of the field. In this case, they found me, as I was an alternate for that year's Open and on-site, so I accepted the invitation to play with David Edwards as a marker.

Perhaps the following tale reflects a bit of youth's freewheeling indiscretions, or maybe I've always been part entertainer at heart, but, on the very first hole I decided I'd hit my driver from off of my knees. The fans absolutely loved it, and it didn't seem to disturb David, as I striped the ball 250 yards from that posture. I did it again on number ten, because, as was the case on number one, it was the perfect shot for that hole (and a fan wanted to get a picture of me doing it). I could hit the ball nice and low that way, the shot would go longer than the 2-iron, and I could hit it more consistently than I could with my 3-wood at that particular time, which is what I most often hit on the first and tenth at Inverness. Besides, it was a legal shot, so I didn't see a problem playing it (and I parred both holes). It's true that I had conveniently forgotten that USGA officer P. J. Boatwright, who approached us riding in his white golf cart like the morally impeccable sheriff in an old Western movie, had asked me to discontinue what he obviously experienced as golf's version of a sacrilegious genuflection. To the disapproving hoots of the crowd, I obliged and, after my second knee drive, finished the round dutifully upright. I won't say that I felt ashamed of my antics, because I really didn't, but what I can confess is that, until now, I never imagined that the episode would re-emerge for the sake of teaching lag (and a forward swing bottom) in a book.

As I said, I was hitting the ball from my knees almost as far (and certainly as solidly) as I did while standing, and, in my prime, I consistently finished in the top 10 percent in driving distance while on tour. Don't forget, I was using a persimmon-headed, steel-shafted driver and a wound balata ball, let alone with no feet or legs!

The point here is, that, instead of driving my swing bottom forward and thus creating lag with my feet and legs, I relied on establishing a clear, forward-aiming point well out in front of my ball, and an aggressive forward shoulder and torso hip-turning motion to create the lag in my swing. Think of it this way: Because a club swung from the knees travels on a far more horizontal, or level-to-the-ground, arc than does one swung while standing up, the bottom, or low point, of such a swing also extends considerably more forward of the ball. Because this makes it easy to swing the club downward through and past the golf ball after impact, such a swing facilitates very solid contact as well. Certainly, it takes some time to get used to the initially awkward posture and geometry of hitting balls from the knees, but once done, you can really pound a golf ball that way.

Needless to say, the feet and legs add extra speed to the golf swing; but they become useless if they don't carry the hips and shoulders forward, to sustain the lag through the impact zone. I credit my efficient lag, created from the hips and shoulders, for driving the ball 250 yards, straight down the fairway. That means the feet and legs only had an additional 15 or 20 yards to give. A final word on this, though: Don't try hitting balls from your knees, on your home course or in tournament play. Officials today seem to have even less of a sense of humor than they did back in 1979!

At the ripe old age of twenty-two, I led during the first three rounds of the 1982 British Open. But then I drove the ball into the pot bunker on the sixth hole, during the third round at Royal Troon, and took three to get out, which led to my precipitous slide down and off of the leader board for good that week. Perhaps that event is somewhat fresh in my mind, because I revisited the scene and recreated my travails as part of an instructional segment for a TNT telecast of the 2004 British Open, on which I worked as a commentator. While my struggles to extricate myself from that bunker back in eighty-two had to do with my inexperience in playing that kind of shot, the reason I found myself in that sandy predicament in the first place had everything to do with my swing dynamics. As I've repeated many times, lag is elusive by nature—just a miniscule uncocking of the left wrist sends it cascading away, and possibly never to be retrieved in that swing again.

Indeed, lag eluded me on my tee shot on the sixth hole, for the simple reason that I didn't load the club well on the backswing. The result was a pull-hook into that infamous bunker. I spoke about how tension in the hands, wrists, and throughout the body restricts and even prevents the free and full loading of the club, and perhaps that culprit tension got the better of me on that swing. As I said, I was only twenty-two.

The somewhat painful phrase, "He threw away the British Open," that people seem to have settled on to encapsulate my woes on that hole, had everything to do with the dynamic-killer of "throwing away" my lag prematurely on that swing.

Rather than replaying my bunker shot during that 2004 TNT segment, I thought about going back to the tee, to explain the flaw in that swing that caused all that trouble. However, while teaching the dynamics of loading and lag would have been a far more useful lesson than one on pitching the ball out of that pot bunker sideways, it would have made for less compelling television. Therefore, I'm glad that I can tell what really happened that day, and that, in emphasizing the danger inherent in poor loading, leading to the loss of lag, something good has emerged from what has remained a bit of a thorn in my memory for all of these years.

To insure that you, the reader, don't repeat my mistake, I'd like to guide you through a little visualization exercise to improve your lag dynamic: Picture your swing, with the lag angle increasing, as the club starts into the downswing. Your fingers are firm on the club, but your wrists are free and relaxed. Your hips initiate the downswing with a blend of a forward shift toward the target and a turn, which helps to sustain this increased angle as long as you can on the downswing. In other words, you never let the lag go—*never let the left wrist begin to uncock even the smallest amount,* because once it begins to uncock it keeps going, throwing lag away with it. The great Byron Nelson has said that you can never release the club too late in the downswing, which means you never want to throw your lag away. Of course, Byron did such a great job of this, they named, and indeed, *modeled* the workings of the mechanical hitting machine, the Iron Byron, after his swing.

Throwing away your lag like this is like dumping all your groceries onto the living room floor before getting them to the kitchen: You'll have nothing to cook when you get to the stove!

Right from the top of your backswing, you want to reengage your faithful friend, the aiming point technique, by aiming your hands at a point well in front of the ball on your target line. As you approach the impact zone, you simply "ride" your pivot motion

through to the end of the swing, without making any conscious adjustment for hitting the ball. It's as if you were to visualize the ball as a soap bubble, and your fully loaded and lagged club swings right through it. Making effective use of the aiming point technique has the added benefit of keeping your hands moving forward of the trailing or lagging club, and I said that one of lag's defining traits is that the club trails the hands right through the impact zone.

The very fact that you have loaded the club so well on the backswing pays out a handsome dividend on the downswing, because loading the club essentially sets the weight of the club head *behind* your hands. Not only does this create the lag angle between your hands and the club shaft, it also means that you have nothing in front of you to slow down your body pivot, as you deliver your club to the ball. It's as if loading the club clears away a mound of debris in front of you, so that your body is free to flow unencumbered in the downswing, right through the impact zone.

A good question I'm often asked is: "If I increase lag on the downswing, won't I have a tendency to flip or turn the club face over too much at the bottom of the swing at impact?"

There is no question that I have seen people with good lag almost panic and flip, or turn the club over too early at the bottom of the swing. But I have seen many more people with little lag flip

or roll it over at the bottom. One of the reasons all golfers struggle with sustaining the lag is that they haven't trained their work-horse, the pivot, to deliver their lag forward enough through the impact zone.

Regardless of your amount of lag, the straightening of the lag angle by the uncocking of the left wrist must be delayed for as long as possible, via a good downswing pivot. The longer it is delayed, the greater the stored power your swing releases into the ball. Furthermore, the more lag we've sustained, the farther forward the swing bottom becomes, and the more the left hip can rotate at the bottom of the swing to maximize the lower body's contribution to the generation of club head speed through the impact zone when you need it most.

Let me clarify the meaning of the term "release." While you never want to release your lag, you certainly do want to allow centrifugal force to release the angles of your cocked left wrist and your bent right arm, because therein lies your swing's power. Again, lag acts as the delivery system of that power.

The more you retain your lag, and the more smoothly you let your pivot move you forward, the later the straightening release of these angles will occur—and the later the better! In fact, from the line of sight of your eyes while making your downswing, everything but your right foot and shoulder appear forward of

the ball, as you swing through the impact zone. Now you see why my writing partner calls the impact zone swing an "optimistic," or forward-looking swing!

Again, your number-one job is not to interfere with the natural physics of centrifugal force, which will release the club (but not the lag) automatically. Maintaining your grip with strong fingers but relaxed wrists helps immeasurably in doing so. The proper feel of sustaining lag is that it has no release point at all until well past impact.

I'm actually appalled by the number of golf instructors today who teach reducing the lag in the swing by having their students release their angles and the club gradually, starting from the top of the swing into the ball.

What's the purpose of teaching that? Any attempt to reduce lag just makes the swing less dynamic. If your goal in golf is to hit the ball shorter with less control, then go ahead and reduce your lag.

Another way to increase lag in your swing is to improve your tempo in the transition of the backswing to the downswing. If your tempo is too slow—that's right, too slow—you will not create enough momentum in the swing to effectively create lag on the downswing. This is another way of saying that you need a relatively quick transition move from the top of the backswing to the start of the downswing. I know this sounds contrary to every

Pages 96–99: Phil Mickelson has a model transition in his swing. Note how, even though the club is well past parallel at the top (more of a style issue), Phil gets the club fully loaded. We can measure that angle between his right wrist and the club shaft at 110 degrees. Phil then lags the club on the "trigger finger" pressure point, keeps his wrists free and relaxed, and initiates his downswing with his lower body, resulting in lag, which increases his angle to 145 degrees. In other words, his body's pivot is beginning to function as the workhorse, leading his dynamics toward the impact zone. *(Photos by Warren Keating. Used with the permission of the PGA Tour and CBS Sports.)*

tip you read that says you should start your downswing slowly and gradually let it gain speed as it proceeds. Again, if you want to decrease your lag, and your power and accuracy with it, start your downswing transition slowly.

When I purposely exaggerate a too-slow transition, my swing bottom invariably gets behind where it needs to be through the impact zone. Then my divots become much shorter, whose centers are two instead of the desired four inches in front of the ball, and I don't feel the sensation of those solidly struck shots. Instead, my impact occurs with more of an uncomfortable vibration rather than that satisfying *thud*. In addition, when I carry this thought of a slow swing transition onto the course, I'm consistently coming up a half- to a full-club short of the hole.

I'm not saying that you should rush the transition without a sense of rhythm, because when my swing tempo is *too* abrupt or fast during the transition of the swing I don't have the time to create enough momentum in my club head to create lag in the first place. I like the analogy of the fly-fisherman who frustratingly tries to cast his line too quickly, and doesn't wait for the line to fully get behind the rod at the top of his cast. He or she has not created load and lag in the lure and cannot possibly deliver it forward effectively. So, the blend you want is a transition that's fast enough to create and sustain lag, but not so fast that it destroys the steady and rhythmic motion of your swing through the impact zone.

Examine a bit more closely just what you learn from accomplished fishermen about sustaining lag in the golf swing: As they "swing" their rods back in preparing to cast, fishermen cannot really feel the line and lure. But the moment they make that change of direction, and the rod begins to move forward, suddenly the lure exerts a weight against the tackle and the fishermen really feel that weight *lagging* behind. Where do they feel it, specifically? Right on that pressure point located across the middle joint of their right forefinger (assuming they are right-handed fishermen, of course).

In fact, it's one of those sad ironies of the game that, in golf, the term "casting" has taken on a negative connotation and meaning, as it has come to denote a premature uncocking of the wrists and the

throwing away of lag. However, the truth of the matter remains that a dynamic swing that creates and conserves lag resembles an accomplished fisherman's casting action with rods and lures. Fishermen most definitely feel that dynamic action in their hands.

The moral of this fishy tale is that every swing wants to achieve its optimum tempo, which invariably is fluid, smooth, and yet effectively strong in storing the energy in the lagging club head. Yet, teaching how to achieve optimum tempo is difficult because, in the final analysis, tempo is experienced as your own subjective feel. Therefore, what you want to do is translate the mechanics of creating lag into your own subjective feel as quickly as you can.

When I am specifically working on achieving optimum tempo to increase my lag, I like to take full practice swings (without the presence of a ball) with a long iron (a 2-, 3-, 4-, or 5-iron or, better yet, a hybrid). Such a middle-length club is a good balance between the driver and the wedge. I work on creating that full load going back, increasing the stress of the shaft and lag on the

The backswing is loaded and looks good, but having a loaded club on the backswing doesn't automatically insure sustaining the lag on the downswing. Here Bobby throws the lag away on the downswing, instantly turning his swing into that of a 40 handicapper. *(Photos by Kerry Corcoran.)*

downswing, delaying the release of the cocking of the wrists before impact, and ripping into the ground, taking a healthy divot. Though I'm not the best friend of the greens superintendent, I'm helping my game the most. If I worry about taking the divot and ruining the grass, I'll move to a more discrete place in the rough, or in a bunker, and do the same thing.

A third option is to take an "air divot" by starting your iron swing six or seven inches off the ground (or carpet). Focus on swinging down and forward of that point, without hitting the ground, through the impact zone. No doubt whoever mows your back lawn will lobby for option number three.

My last word on tempo is that, when I achieve my optimum tempo in the transition of the swing, I create more force through the impact zone, a flat left wrist, a forward swing bottom, and a longer divot with a more forward bottom or center point. In other words, my swing displays better dynamics across the board, and, oh, how I love how that feels!

The grip also has a role in sustaining and increasing lag. We introduced the role of grip pressure in our pitching section, and since golf is a difficult and complicated game already, there's no need to complicate matters even more by suggesting a different grip for the full shot than for other standard-grip shots. However, you'll want to remember that the two hands with which you grip the club are the only parts of your body that ever touch the club, and that both hands play a major role in setting, or loading, storing, and lagging the club correctly.

More specifically, you want to be aware that the club is set and loaded via a blended combination of the last three fingers of the left hand gripping, cocking the left thumb upward, and the backward bending of the right wrist. The right hand is as important as the left in loading the club, because, if you lose that good connection with the club that the right hand provides, your hands separate on the club, making it more difficult to load the club fully. As you know, a club that is not fully loaded struggles to retain its lag during the downswing.

Again, it is *absolutely essential* that both wrists remain relaxed and free throughout the swing. You want to apply a little extra pressure in those last three fingers on the left hand, because that hand needs to be structurally solid enough to support the forceful blow of impact, and to insure a flat left wrist through the impact zone, and you can never be too mentally conscious of the importance of the flat left wrist at impact. The more aware you are, and the more you visualize a flat left wrist at impact *before you even begin to make your swing,* the greater your chances of achieving it during an actual swing.

In fact, I've talked already about the drill of shifting from the address to the impact position, i.e., from the club centered on the body and the left wrist bent, to the shaft leaning forward and the left wrist flat, and to do this back and forth, a couple of times in a row. This is a great way of ingraining a mental image of the difference between address and impact.

Whether you interlock, overlap, or use a ten-finger grip, really falls into the category of style. Though I use the traditional overlap grip myself, I don't have any problem with anyone using the interlocking grip. I guess it can't be too bad, if it has worked so well for the two best players the game has ever known, Jack Nicklaus and Tiger Woods. I do have a little reservation, however, with using the ten-finger grip, as I believe that, because this grip separates the hands on the club more than the others, it could potentially make it more difficult to load and lag the club. But in reality, some players, like Bob Rosburg (Rossy, a great player during the Arnold Palmer era, continues to work as a TV golf commentator), have had good careers using the ten-finger grip. Bob Estes has been known to change from the overlap to the ten-finger grip from time to time. In fact, Bob Estes won the 2001 Federal Express-St. Jude Classic in Memphis using a ten-finger grip.

Some players have displayed wonderful imaginations in creating their own unique grips, such as Jim Furyk, who double-overlaps both the pinky and ring fingers of his right hand on top of his left. Or consider Steve Jones, who was bold enough to use the reverse overlap grip on his full swings (where we've previously almost exclusively seen it used for putting), after his biking accident in the early nineties. Using the normal overlapping grip (with the right pinky draped over the left forefinger) prevented Steve's injured finger from healing. After being out of competitive golf for three years, Steve used his new grip to win the 1996 U.S. Open at Oakland Hills, outside of Detroit, in what I feel was one of the most underrated achievements in the history of the game. In fact, one day when Steve was just returning to competitive golf, we were hitting balls together at my house (I had my own driving range in the backyard at the time); he was showing me his grip change and, after asking me to give it a try, he instantly turned me into a 15 handicapper, as I couldn't believe how far to the right I hit the ball!

Whatever grip style you choose, you want the hands to work together as a single unit, or as a "corporate" entity, as Ben Hogan called it. The key to doing so is to make sure that your hands do not shift their position through the swing because of a change in grip pressure.

A really good grip is indeed a work of art. They used to say that Seve Ballesteros looked like he was born with a golf club in his hands. Ben Crenshaw's hands appear as if they were molded right onto the club. Arnold Palmer's father, Deacon, or "Deke," a PGA club pro, placed young Arnie's hands on the club correctly, then said, "Son, don't move them from there, and go out and play!"

Some tour players have so obsessed with gripping the club correctly that, rumor has it, they sleep with a club near their beds, so they can wake up in the middle of the night to practice their grips.

Now let's look at what I would argue is one of the most

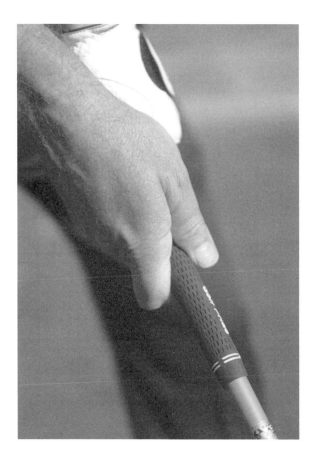

A sound grip is fundamental to creating good dynamics. *(Photo by Kerry Corcoran.)*

overlooked, if not *the* most overlooked fundamental of the golf swing, that point of pressure created by the club resting against and across the middle joint of the right hand's forefinger. This pressure point transforms that finger into what is commonly called "the trigger finger," and plays a major role in loading the club on the backswing and lagging it on the downswing. It is there, where the club shaft falls against the finger, that we feel the resistance of the club, as it goes through its transition from backswing to downswing.

This "trigger-finger pressure point" applies pressure from the joint in the middle knuckle to the aft, or back, side of the grip and greatly contributes to the amount of power you can apply into the ball at impact. What's more, A golfer cannot *feel* the golf club through the swing in any place other than their hands, and it is against the right forefinger's pressure point that the golfer feels lag during the downswing and right through the impact zone. In fact, as you become more proficient in loading and lagging the club against your right forefinger, you will begin to feel, in a very real sense, that your hands and the club head have become equivalents. In other words, you literally feel the club head in your hands, which is why, at several places in this book, I've said that we want "our minds to be in our hands." But this kind of direct monitoring and communication between the club head and the hands takes a little time to develop.

Here's what I often do with my amateur playing partners who do not have a well-established forefinger pressure point on the club: I ask them to go to the top of their backswing position, take their right forefinger and thumb off the grip completely, and poise there. I then put a little weight on their club head by pulling down on it a bit. What happens is that, without a well-established forefinger pressure point, their club head sinks straight down because there is nothing there to support it. Now, I teach them to grip the club correctly, by laying the handle diagonally across that middle joint of their trigger finger. Now, when poised at the top of their backswing, I put the same tug and weight on their club head as I did before, and that pressure point resists and supports the club, and does not let it droop down out of control at all.

During the swing itself, you want to allow the weight of the golf club to fall right against that trigger-finger pressure point, as your means of completing the backswing's loading motion, which then makes lagging the club on the downswing possible. Virtually all tour player's finish loading their club this way, perhaps most visibly noticeable in the swings of Sergio Garcia, Rory Sabatini, Chad

Campbell, Bart Bryant, Jason Gore, Lucas Glover, and Kenny Perry, among others.

After you've loaded your lag into the forefinger pressure point, you want to feel the weight of the club itself lie there and retain its heavy and inert feeling, all the way down through the impact zone.

I've talked a lot about the pivot, and now I want to offer a word of caution about it here: It can be counterproductive to teach the pivot, if the pro omits the pivot's link to, and role in, creating good swing dynamics. I have watched a countless number of golfers who have taken tons and tons of lessons, and many have a beautiful-looking pivot. Yet, few improve from being 23 handicappers. Why? The reason is that they all still have lousy dynamics. Of course, their teaching pros become more and more frustrated, because they are at their wits' end about what to teach them anymore.

I can stand stock-still, not use my body, and still hit the ball with good dynamics. I can put my feet together and hit the ball, or I can hit the ball from my knees, and have great dynamics. There's very little pivot on a chip shot, but, nevertheless, when executed correctly, it displays the dynamics of a flat left wrist and a forward swing bottom.

I was talking to a man I met at a business function recently. He said he has taken so many lessons over the years, then added, "What do I have to show for it?" He says his claim to fame among his buddies is that he's the world's worst golfer with a very good golf swing. What he meant to say was "a very good-*looking* golf swing," because he evidently had the style components of the swing down pat. All that money he poured into golf lessons had bought him nothing more than a stylish swing. Combined with his sharp clothes, pro golf bag, and top-of-the-line clubs, he certainly played the part of a golfer. His frustration was rooted in the fact that his golf teacher overlooked teaching him the swing's dynamics during all of those pivot-centered lessons.

A swing with a beautiful pivot, but no dynamics, is like a beautiful bottle with no wine in it! We must use the pivot solely to deliver and support our dynamics.

It's time for a moment of full disclosure. We've been speaking repeatedly about how poor dynamics slows the club down and releases it too soon, and into the ground behind the ball. The surprising truth is all golfers, from Ben Hogan to Hulk Hogan, actually strike the ball with the club in a decelerating mode. Maximum acceleration occurs in all swings prior to impact to varying degrees of distance. Physics dictates that, though golfers certainly do express a "true" feeling, when they insist that they are accelerating the club through impact and past the ball, their club speed actually slows down as it approaches impact. By learning to develop good swing dynamics, aided by a sound pivot, you can move that point of maximum acceleration as close to the ball as you can, and achieve as much effective acceleration through the impact zone as humanly possible. That's what the best players in the world do: They're slowing down *closer to the ball* than their high-handicap friends and playing partners.

Let me tell you the story of when I first met Ben Hogan, as it speaks right to this point of the pivot's function in transporting our dynamics into and forward of the ball in as much an accelerating manner as possible: It was 1981, and I was having trouble getting the club shaft sufficiently forward at impact, which meant that my swing bottom wasn't sufficiently forward of the ball. I had noticed in my swing videos that my right elbow was digging into my side on my downswing, and not driving ahead of the ball, as Mr. Hogan's did in his swing. My good friend, Mark O'Meara, arranged for me to meet with Mr. Hogan in his legendary Fort Worth office, where I asked the great man if he would kindly suggest something that would remedy this problem for me. He said that the key to getting that right hand and arm forward was to turn the hips through impact as aggressively as possible.

I can still hear his confident voice speaking those words:

"You cannot turn your hips fast enough through impact." Indeed, Mr. Hogan's suggestion helped me begin to strike the ball more dynamically, but only after I realized that I needed to load stronger on the backswing and lag stronger on the downswing. Otherwise, the quick-moving hips would cause me to swing over the top. It was at that moment that I began to feel the wonderful way the swing's dynamics interact and support one another, because, as I said earlier in this chapter, efficient loading clears the way for the body's pivot to lag the club through the impact zone. The week after my meeting with Mr. Hogan, I placed second at the Westchester Classic, and then went on to finish fourteenth on the PGA Tour money list that year, and had my best season ever.

During that week at Westchester, who do you think came running across the parking lot looking to talk to me? It was none other than Gary Player, who somehow had gotten word that I had procured that rarest commodity of all in the golf world, a private session with Mr. Hogan.

"Bobby, Bobby," I can still hear Gary cry out with that inimitable enthusiasm, tinged with his South African accent. "What did Mr. Hogan tell you?" I was happy to share with him the conversation I just shared with you. Though, perhaps the fact that Gary has always transferred his weight so well through the impact zone—so much so, in fact, that he often lets his right foot cross over and forward of his left after impact—explains why he showed something significantly less than excitement after hearing the specifics of Mr. Hogan's "lesson."

Let me tell you another Hogan story that further supports the importance of blending a good pivot and good swing dynamics: Mr. Hogan once sat down with my stepdad, the late Fletcher Jones, and put a sugar cube on a table, then said: "The key to the golf swing is that, on the through swing, you want to hit the inside corner of that sugar cube."

What he was saying was that when you've loaded the club

properly, and sustained that load through lagging the club on the downswing, you will automatically hit the ball (which the sugar cube represented) from the inside. The reason why people hit the ball (and a sugar cube, too, were they to swing at one) from the outside, which produces a slice, is that they let go of their lag too soon (if they ever even created it in the first place). And the reason they do this is usually because they didn't load the club well in the backswing.

In other words, a swing path that approaches the ball from the inside produces that nice, gentle draw that indicates an accomplished golfer; but the instant one throws their lag away, the club head begins to orbit down into the impact zone on an "outside-to-in" path, and such a downswing causes a slice, a pull, or a pull hook.

As a golf commentator, I've been watching the best players in the world hit golf shots, week after week, for over fifteen years. I've gotten to the point that I know exactly where the player has hit the shot without looking at the ball flight, but just by watching the efficiency of his dynamics through impact. I can see how efficiently they load and lag the club, or if they lose that lag, or throw it away before impact. I can also tell the quality of the shot by the sound of the strike at impact, as those hit with good dynamics sound far better (again, a true *thud* or *crack*, versus a weak *clink*). I only do swing analysis during my job assignments with TNT (the British Open, PGA, Grand Slam, and President's Cup), so viewers won't get much of me doing commentary on players' swings, but it's been a pretty amazing transformation for me.

In fact, I have to resist the temptation to predict a shot's outcome while the ball is still in the air. Frank Chirkinian, the godfather of golf on television, the man who gave me my start at CBS and was my mentor, would often yell at me in my headset, "Damn it, Clampett, how many times do I have to tell you? Don't call shots in the air!" The truth is I'm much better at translating my perception of a swing's dynamics into a description of the shape and quality of the shot now, than when I began in broadcasting, which means the effort to remain silent has become tougher, too.

However, watching all those swings, both live from my broadcast booth and on the television monitor, has helped me both to better understand my own swing and to communicate my thoughts in writing. (Of course, it helps having a great coauthor like Andy!)

What many amateurs notice is that the pull shot version of this throwing-the-lag-away problem occurs more with the wedges and short iron shots, and that the pulls turn into slices with their less-lofted clubs, meaning the long irons, fairway woods, and driver. What's more, losing lag often results in erratic distance control, so a golfer may hit his or her pitching wedge and short irons longer than normal (say, a 130-yard shot with a pitching wedge), and their long irons relatively too short (a 180-yard shot with a 3-iron, for example). On the other hand, players capable of loading and lagging the club well are likely to hit their wedge shots 120 yards and their 3-iron shots 210 yards, which represents a more consistent yardage gap between all of the irons in their set.

Manufacturers are continually building "hooks" into their metalwood clubs by producing them with shut faces to counteract club head throwaway (more on this in our equipment chapter), but treating the problem this way doesn't make it go away completely. In fact, a golfer's out-to-in slice swing often becomes a bigger pull, or pull hook, with the modern club specs, because the built-in, closed club faces make the balls that start left fly and/or hook even more to the left, whereas the same swing with an "old-fashioned" square-club-faced wood would allow shots that start to the left to slice back toward the target. Sadly, many golfers are content with this solution, but it doesn't improve their handicaps. They could all improve their games far more soundly, the moment they begin to improve their swing dynamics through the impact zone.

Let's talk a bit about Mr. Hogan's alleged secret. Perhaps we should refer to it as *one of* his alleged secrets, because people have speculated that he had a number of them. The secret I have in mind, however, involved Mr. Hogan's backswing, and the fact that, at its top, he allegedly fanned, or rotated, the club face to a more opened position. (Remember, in his earlier days as a pro, Mr. Hogan struggled mightily with a hook.) What this slight act of rotation also did, was to direct and drop that club right down on his forefinger pressure point, across the middle joint of his index finger, the very location of which marks that point where lag is felt, stored, and sustained right through the impact zone. In other words, Mr. Hogan's secret, and the dynamic that Homer Kelley deemed the secret of golf in *The Golfing Machine*, were one and the same thing—which is, of course, lag.

Shifting gears just a bit, let's recall the great Sam Snead, who once said: "Hit the driver on the downswing!"

The truth is that I'm blown away by the fact that so many "reputable" golf teachers (not to mention books and magazine articles) instruct their students to strike their driver on the upswing! *Nothing could be farther from the truth! Don't listen to them!* Have I made my point clear? Regardless of whether a ball is on a tee or on the ground in the fairway, regardless of what club you are using, the swing bottom must consistently be four inches in front of the ball, to achieve maximum efficiency and consistency. Swinging slightly down on the ball with the driver goes a long way toward insuring a flat left wrist at impact, because, as soon as the club begins to swing up and in, there is a tendency for the left wrist to break down and cup, destroying its flat alignment.

Some instructors try to hedge their bets, or disguise their own ignorance about the subject by saying that the driver should be moving on a level path when it strikes the ball. While this is better than advising students to hit up on the ball with the driver, I still have a big problem with the suggestion, and here's why: Golfers swing all of their clubs in a circular arc, so there is no *level* section anywhere in the swing; the club moves either up or down. If it isn't moving down during the swing (which a level motion obviously doesn't describe), then it's moving up. And they say golf isn't rocket science!

I can understand how the swing may *feel* level through impacting the ball with the driver, because the ball is on a tee, and the golfer may sense the club swinging parallel to the ground below the tee; but our Swing Vision photos of driver shots through the impact zone confirm that the best players in the world *do* swing slightly down on the ball with their drivers. I think it's better to be clear on the path of the club through the ball with the driver, that is to say, slightly downward, and to cultivate that feeling and sensation through the impact zone.

Of course, even these players make poor swings occasionally; so I wouldn't be disclosing all of the evidence, if I didn't say that we saw some driver shots struck on the upswing. What I am not able to report is the results of such shots, but my strong suspicion is that they did not produce the best drives.

Note that the path of Phil Mickelson's driver is decisively downward as it approaches the ball. *(Photos by Warren Keating. Used with the permission of the PGA Tour and CBS Sports.)*

To prove my point that we have better dynamics when swinging slightly down on the ball with the driver, I went to the driving range and hit fifty drives with my normal ball position, and with my swing bottom four inches in front of the ball. Then I hit another fifty drives after moving the ball forward three inches in my stance, with my swing bottom two inches behind the ball, which I accomplished by drawing my aiming point back. The results of the second group of drives were an 18-yard loss of distance and a 7-yard loss of accuracy.

You may argue, "Bobby, you needed a driver with specs designed for the swing bottom being behind the ball, meaning a more game-improvement type of driver than I normally play. Such a club would have more loft, its weight positioned lower and deeper in the club head. So I went and got the best driver of this kind that I could find—and I was still 7 yards more off-line with it, but I only lost 8 yards of distance. In other words, the game-improvement driver did its compensating work for a poor swing bottom and restored some distance, but it couldn't solve the accuracy problem that swinging up on the ball created.

Of course, the best drivers of the ball, such as Vijay Singh, combine excellent distance and accuracy. In fact, according to the PGA Tour stats, Vijay has ranked in the top five in total driving in his last eight seasons. That's consistency! He has so much confidence with the driver, that he uses it where other players hit irons off the tee, on short and tight par-4 holes.

His faith in his driving ability was never more evident than at the 1998 PGA Championship at Sahalee Golf Club, near Seattle, Washington, when he came to the fifteenth hole in the final round with a one-stroke lead over Steve Stricker. I was covering the hole for CBS, and most players, including Steve Stricker, were hitting an iron off the tee, as the fairway narrowed to a 15-yard landing area for the majority of drives. Vijay proceeded to hit a perfect drive, bisected the fairway, made birdie, and went on to win his first major championship. I should also mention that

Steve also birdied the hole laying up, when he stuck a 7-iron stiff to the flag stick.

As you can extrapolate from this Swing Vision photo of Vijay at impact, his swing bottom with the driver is well forward of the ball. He has so much confidence with his driver swing, that he often even hits the club off the fairway, where striking down on the ball becomes an imperative.

I also covered the 2005 Shell Houston Open at the Redstone Golf Club, for CBS. Vijay was again in the final group the last two days (what else is new?), and I spent some time with him on the driving range. I love watching Vijay practice, especially observing how he works in his drills hitting balls. He often uses his weighted club to do drills, and he even hits practice balls with it. During this practice session, Vijay was hitting many drivers "off the deck."

Now, the grass on this practice tee was mowed down to a height of around three-eighths of an inch, like a tee box, i.e., shorter than on an actual fairway. Vijay, at the time, played a large, 400-cc R7 driver from TaylorMade, and as he positioned the club

One can clearly see that Vijay is striking his driver on the downswing, evidenced by his forward-leaning club shaft at impact. His swing bottom is close to four inches in front of the ball. (Photo by Warren Keating. Used with the permission of the PGA Tour and CBS Sports.)

behind the ball, the center of the ball lined up with the second groove of the driver. The sweet spot on the R7 is the fourth groove up, so Vijay was making contact with the ball two grooves below the sweet spot, yet he still hit beautiful, high-flying shots of about 280 yards. Vijay could hit these sorts of fairway driver shots, only because he had good swing dynamics, with a forward swing bottom. If his swing bottom was behind the ball, he would not have been able to get those driver shots off the ground and up into the air. In fact, Vijay likes to practice hitting drivers off of the ground, and not off a tee, *specifically because* it makes him move his swing bottom in front of the ball.

For the same reason, I recommend that you give this practice drill a try. Remember however, none of us are Vijay Singh, meaning that it takes a lot of club head speed to launch drivers off of the ground and high into the air. Therefore, work with your driver on moving the bottom of your swing arc forward of the ball, and consider shots lofted to a reasonable height (i.e., lower than ones hit off of a tee) as a sign of your improved swing dynamics.

Later in the 2005 season, I was covering the PGA Grand Slam of Golf, at the beautiful Hyatt Poipu Bay on Kauai. Vijay was struggling with his game and missing many fairways and greens. In fact, he finished last of the four players, who included Tiger Woods (who won his sixth Grand Slam), Phil Mickelson, and Michael Campbell. After the event I met up with Vijay, and we had an opportunity to talk about his swing and why he was hitting so many shots to the right with his driver and fairway woods, as well as hitting fat and thin shots with his irons. In fact, during the first round of the competition he hit two balls in the water on the par-3 eleventh hole and made a triple bogie. That wasn't the *real* Vijay Singh, in my opinion, and, certainly not in his, either.

When I mentioned that I noticed that his swing bottom had a tendency to fall behind the ball, he listened very intently. I also shared my thought that his swing looked like it was getting stuck behind him on his downswing, and that the cause was nothing more than his swing bottom falling too far back, i.e., not in its normal location, four inches in front of the ball. Vijay then began to tell me how he had gotten away from practicing a strong weight shift through the ball. He said that it had been a while since he'd practiced hitting long irons and fairway woods off an uphill lie, which makes up a drill he devised specifically to get his weight to his left side while moving through the impact zone. (This also a very good drill to train the pivot to transport lag and load, as well as bringing your swing bottom correctly forward of the ball, because, if you can get your swing bottom consistently in front on a significant uphill lie, you've got it down—so to speak.)

I then introduced him to the aiming point technique, which he had never heard of, and I explained how to execute it in the exact same way as I have taught it to you, the reader, in this book. He promised he would go and practice it, then later admitted that it helped him. It had to, because moving the aiming point forward brought his swing bottom forward, and thus eliminated that awful feeling he had of getting the club stuck behind his body on the downswing.

Sam Snead was right: Hitting the ball on the upswing is a great way to impose havoc on your game. A forward swing bottom will always lead to better swing dynamics, and it will produce more power and more accuracy in your swing, for all shots, *including* with the driver.

FULL SWING AND LAG DRILLS

The Full Swing Sand Drill

Lest you think I've forgotten, we still have one more lesson to learn in our practice sand bunker. You will use a 5- or 6-iron this time, and draw that line in the sand, addressing it as if it were the ball positioned where we would an actual ball. Take some full swings, while concentrating on loading the club fully on the backswing, and lagging the club, with that load sustained, all the way through the downswing. Look to see that your sand divot falls in front of that line.

If it has, great! If not, work on the following things: Move that line (again, the ball's proxy) back a little in your stance (but never more than about four inches inside the left heel), and make sure you have loaded and set the club completely, with a full cocking of the left wrist. Make a complete pivot behind the ball on the backswing, and execute a blend of slide and turn, all the way through the impact zone. Continue to strive to upgrade these elements of your full swing, and that divot will fall in front of the line before you know it. Pay close attention to specifically where in relation to the line your club enters the sand when you make poor versus well-loaded and -lagged swings.

Most people making a full swing struggle with the sand drill at first, then they start to catch on but are inconsistent, in terms of repeating this forward-of-the-line center of their divot. Next, after becoming consistent in striking the sand in front of the line without a ball, they find that, with a ball, their forward divot location still remains inconsistent.

You guessed it! The ball has captured the golfer's attention, which has caused a movement of the bottom of the swing back from its four-inch-forward goal.

If this describes your efforts, don't fret, as you're in the company of the majority of golfers. Continue to do your sand drill, both with and without a ball; but when you are hitting a ball from the sand, maintain your focus on the aiming point in front of the line, just as you would on swings without the ball. Remember, it takes a little time and practice to retrain your mind to direct the club to the aiming point, and not to the ball, but stay with it and you'll succeed. In fact, though you will have moved your swing bottom a mere four inches in front of the ball, you'll find that your ball-striking and golf game will improve immeasurably.

The sand drill can be even more effective from an uphill lie (see Vijay's drill below), and the greater the angle of uphill, the more your pivot will have to work to attain your desired forward swing bottom. This is an exceptional way to practice.

LAG DRILLS

Here are a couple of helpful drills that are designed to improve and increase your club head lag. . . .

Let me take you back to my early years as a junior golfer. I was thirteen years old and had just begun taking golf instruction from Ben Doyle. I had never heard of the lag concept, though Ben instantly had me working on increasing my lag. He showed me the usefulness of loading and lagging the club on the forefinger pressure point, and then sent me into a vacant lot, with foot-high grass, to ingrain it in my swing. Using a short iron, I would swing through the long grass with great force, feeling the loading of the club on the backswing and the lagging of the club on the downswing. The long grass would act as a resistance against the club as it went through the impact zone, and this resistance both sustained and ingrained in my hands and body the feeling of lag.

In addition, the grass's resistance strengthened my arms, wrists, and hands, and soon I was better able to support my improving swing dynamics. I would then take this feel to the driving range when hitting balls. When Ben and I viewed my filmed swing, the improvement in my loading, and my lag, was immediately evident. After two diligent weeks of drilling in the long grass, my lag move was formed. It's still present in my swing today, thanks to my recommitment to swing dynamics (over swing style). In fact, many call this lag my swing's signature move.

Lag Training Aids

There are several fitness-training devices on the market today that are designed to increase lag and strength. Look for them in golf magazines, online, on Golf Channel infomercials, or ask your pro shop, or local golf shop salesperson to recommend them.

Vijay Singh's Uphill Drill

If this drill is good enough for one of the best players in the world, it makes sense that everyone should give it a try: Find a small hill, preferably pointing downrange, at your practice range. What often works well is the mounding on the side of an elevated practice tee, or practice bunker area, near the tee. If you can't find such a hill or mount oriented the correct way (i.e., downrange, so that your back foot is lower than your front foot at address), use any hill available.

Tee up a ball and take a swing with your driver, making the needed effort to fight the gravity of the upslope, so as to transfer your weight strongly to your left side. As I said, this drill not only improves your forward pivot motion, but your ability to create a forward swing bottom four inches in front of the ball as well. Stick with the driver and a tee with this drill, because, without a tee, the upward slope will have a tendency to deliver your club into the ground directly behind the ball.

BULLET POINTS

- Lag not only belongs to the downswing part of your motion, *it is the downswing's number-one priority, concern, and goal, until you've swung well past the both-arms-straight follow-through position.*

- From a purely descriptive point of view, lag describes the condition of the club head continually trailing the body, arms, and hands, and of course, the club shaft, right up to impact and through. We can also measure lag, and both further define and, indeed, see it as the size of the angle created between the left arm, wrist and hand, and the club shaft.

- In conjunction with learning how to establish lag, you need to work on refining your body's work, meaning your pivot motion. If the power that you lag into impact is your precious cargo, the pivot is the transportation vehicle that carries the goods for you through the impact zone. That is why we call the pivot the golf swing's workhorse.

- One of the criticisms people often made of my swing, when I first came on tour, was that it had too much lag. A writer asked my teacher Ben Doyle whether he thought this was true, and if, indeed, a swing can have too much lag? Ben answered, "Can you have too much love?" meaning that you can't have too much of a good thing.

- The more you retain your lag, and the more smoothly you let your pivot move you forward, the later the straightening release of these angles will occur, and the later the better. In fact, from the line of sight of your eyes, everything but your right foot and shoulder should appear *forward of the ball,* as you swing through the impact zone.

CHAPTER FIVE

THE STRAIGHT PLANE LINE (THROUGH THE IMPACT ZONE):

Dynamic #5— The Guiding Dynamic

Imagine you want to make a dead-straight three-foot putt. How would you go about doing so? First you would stand behind your ball, or otherwise survey the green to visualize a straight target line on the ground between your ball and the center of the cup. Then you would draw your putter back and stroke the ball straight down that line into the hole. Establishing the line of the putt represents one of the two essential fundamentals of the putting game, the other being the speed with which you want to hit your putt along your intended line. Now, because you are rolling the ball along the ground, you have no trouble visualizing and, indeed, literally locating your target line on the ground itself. Once you have established this line, only a crazy golfer would swing the putter in any other direction than straight down that line, right? It sounds obvious, and of course it is.

However, as soon as you walk to the next tee and pull out your driver, you automatically raise your sights, anticipating the flight of the ball, and direct it to a landing point or area often more than 200 yards down the fairway (let's make that more than 300 yards away, for many of today's tour players). Because you are (hopefully) not rolling your drives to that spot, it seems obvious that you wouldn't trace the journey along a line on the ground, as you do a putt. You are right, of course, to a large degree.

If, in the putting chapter I described a putt as a "miniature drive," it's logical to reverse the comparison and talk about a drive as a gigantic, or extended, putt. Granted, doing so requires some imagination, because you hit your drive in the air, not along the ground, and because the longer driver swing completely fills out an arc, or circular shape, that the short putting stroke only begins to trace. However, if somehow you did have a two-hundred-yard putt on the world's largest green, your putting "stroke" would indeed extend into a very conventional-looking full swing.

The point is that with every shot you hit in the game of golf—from three-foot putts to three-hundred-yard drives—you want your club shaft pointing at the straight plane line through impact, along the intended line on which you want your shots to start. Golf may not be a game of "perfect" but it definitely is a game of "straight."

If it were only as easy as that!

Part of the difficulty is that you are trying to hit the ball straight, but with a circular swing. To thicken the plot, this circular swing doesn't occur on a vertical plane that is perpendicular to the ground. If it did, the swinging golf club would resemble the motion of a Ferris wheel, and as the club head reached the bottom of its arc, it would strike the ball and propel it straight as an arrow along the plane of its movement, i.e., straight down the fairway, right at the target.

Instead, the golf swing's circle takes place on an inclined plane that is angled or pitched, very much like a rooftop, with the club shaft at address establishing the initial angle of the inclined plane on which the circular journey of the golf swing begins. Of course, as we shall soon see, the swing's circle, or swing plane, as it is more commonly called, may shift or deviate from its starting angle rather quickly.

If all of this sounds a bit complicated, fear not, as simplifying help lies literally right at your feet, because your angled swing

The straight plane line is our fifth and final dynamic, and it literally guides the motion of our swing from the address to the finish. *(Photo by Kerry Corcoran.)*

plane has a straight baseline. To visualize this idea, take a hard-cover book and place it on a table. Now raise the book up to a 45-degree angle, while the bound spine side of the book remains on the table. It's easy to see that, while the angle of the book cover increases the more you raise the book up, the position of the spine of the book doesn't change at all: It still lies in a straight line on the table. In golf, we call this straight baseline of the inclined plane the "straight plane line" (aka, the "target line"). Just as you see this line when you stand over a three-foot putt, when addressing a full shot, you imagine and visualize this line as if it were literally inscribed along the ground and extended itself through the ball and all the way to the target (even if we don't track it with our eyes all the way there).

This straight plane line becomes our fifth and final swing dynamic, and it literally guides and dictates the motion of our swing, from start to finish. That is why we are calling it "the guiding dynamic."

The only way we can possibly start our golf shot straight along the line on which we intend the ball to fly is to swing our club shaft on the straight plane line through the impact zone. That is to say, the club shaft will point to the plane line. However, because we are standing on one side of the ball, and because we swing our golf club in an angled arc, it is impossible for our club shaft to lit-

erally swing over, or cover, this plane line through most of the impact zone. Rather, swinging on-plane simply means that the club head and shaft approach the ball from inside the straight plane line, while at the same time the club shaft points directly at it, from the instant the club head and shaft swing down past their parallel-to-the-ground alignment until the moment the club makes contact with the golf ball.

At that point, the club head and shaft actually touch the straight plane line for the first time since address. They then swing up and past their parallel-to-the-ground alignment, to the finish of the swing. Again, address and impact represent the only two times during the swing that the club head and shaft actually touch the straight plane line.

Because golf swings on television, and in photographs in books and magazines, appear in two dimensions, people forget the fact that the golf swing actually has three dimensions. It swings back up and in, heading to the top of the swing, and then down, forward, and out toward the ball on the downswing, before swinging forward, in, and up, to the finish. My writing partner,

Though each player has his or her own style of downswing (here, it is Jim Furyk), the fifth dynamic requires that their club shafts all must be on-plane through the impact zone. (Photos by Warren Keating. Used with the permission of the PGA Tour and CBS Sports.)

Andy Brumer, likes to say that because of its volume, the golf swing is really a kinetic sculpture.

The sensory illusion of the golf swing is that even though the club both appears, and, indeed, does move in a circular fashion from inside the straight plane line before impact to inside the straight plane line (again, because the path of the club head is on a tilted arc) after impact, the golfer feels as if he or she is swinging the club straight down the straight plane line, through the impact zone, with the full force of the club head having passed directly through the center of the ball.

As the photographs captured by the Swing Vision camera clearly show, the circular motion of the swinging golf club "draws" a perfect arc through the impact zone, with the straight plane line acting as a solid guide and border, across which the golf club never passes. This is why we are calling the straight plane line our guiding dynamic. I can't emphasize enough the importance of thinking in pictures this way, and we're very lucky, indeed, to have this great Swing Vision technology to sharpen and clarify our focus.

"But Bobby, why are you calling the straight plane line a 'dynamic'?"

Excellent question. Let's begin to answer it by reviewing the definition of the word "dynamic," as we've used it in this book. A swing dynamic involves the efficient creation, storage, and application of

power accurately into the ball. (Also remember that, as these dynamics create maximum power and distance, they also simultaneously create the correct geometric alignments you need to produce maximum accuracy. That's the magic of these dynamics and why they are so essential to playing good golf.)

Now, in addition to your straight plane line through the impact zone, imagine you have a rotated, or a misaligned one that points 30 degrees to the right of both your target and the line on which you want your shot to start. In other words, you now have two plane lines inscribed on the ground, the ideal straight one toward our target, and our misdirected one pointing to the right of it.

This would be fine if, as in baseball, you can swing along this crooked plane line, and hit your golf ball 30 degrees to the right of our target, and still keep the ball in play. However, while 30 degrees off center in baseball may go for a triple in the right field corner, 30 degrees off line in golf will more than likely land the ball in the trees.

You can also turn your straight plane line so that it points left of the target. The problem is that, as you enter the impact zone

As you can see, the club head only touches the straight plane line when it contacts the ball. It then immediately swings back inside of it, though it points to it, until the shaft reaches its parallel-to-the-ground alignment. *(Photos by Warren Keating. Used with the permission of the PGA Tour and CBS Sports.)*

swinging along an angled rather than a straight plane line—
whether it is pointing incorrectly to the left or to the right—you
instinctively (and desperately) try to correct yourself at the last
instant by bending that line, in an attempt to redirect your swing
back toward your straight target line. In other words, you are
swinging in two directions with one swing!

More times than not, you create this incorrectly rotated plane
line by aligning yourself incorrectly to the right or left of your
straight plane line at address. Though experienced golfers can do
this (Lee Trevino aims left, and Gary Player aims right) because
they have the skill to still swing on-plane through the impact
zone, for the purposes of this book, I'm recommending that you
address straight shots with your feet, knees, hips, and shoulders
parallel to your straight plane line.

I've said that you'll know you are "on-plane" through the impact zone when, just prior to and after impact, the shaft points directly at the straight plane line. We know we are off-plane through
the impact zone, then, when our shaft points either beyond the
straight plane line (we say such swings are "over the top" of the
plane), or at a point on the ground inside of the straight plane line
(which we might describe as an "under-the-top" swing).

Of course, golfers are by and large an intelligent group of people, so no one planning on hitting a straight shot intentionally

rotates his or her aiming line away from their target, then bends (meaning changes the direction of) their swing back toward the target. Rather, this more often than not results from the dynamics of load and lag breaking down at the start of the downswing.

When golfers throw away their lag prematurely, from the top of the swing, they immediately lose the angle between their left arm and the club shaft. This leads to an overuse of the hands and wrists, which tosses the club off its circular orbit, and usually redirects it from outside the target line back across it, to the inside. This changes the straight plane line by bending it to the left, and impact becomes a glancing blow that usually imparts a slicing left-to-right spin on the ball.

While it's less common, some golfers can reroute their clubs, so that they approach the impact zone from too far inside the target line. This would bend or reorient their plane lines to the right. The only way a golfer can redirect a swing from off-plane to on-plane, through the impact zone, is by weakly and ineffectually flipping the club back on-line and on-plane with his or her wrists.

Don't look at this swing too long! Note how when the dynamics of load and lag are destroyed, so is the dynamic of the straight plane line, resulting in the "hacker's slice." Also, notice how my left wrist is bent and not flat as it must be at impact.
(Photos by Kerry Corcoran.)

While it's true that the strongest and most talented of golfers can occasionally still hit a good shot this way, most amateurs entering the impact zone with such broken-down dynamics rarely strike down and through the ball with a flat left wrist, a forward-leaning club shaft, and a forward swing bottom well in front of the ball.

Ultimately then, a straight plane line qualifies as our fifth dynamic, simply because swinging in correct relation to it through the impact zone allows golfers to strike the ball with all of their other four dynamics completely intact and uncompromised.

Just as the straight plane line frees the previous four dynamics to work effectively, those very same four dynamics can work together to establish a straight plane line. Here's how and why: A full loading of the club allows you to create power on the back-swing. A well-lagged downswing directs the club toward the straight plane line correctly, from the inside, as it enters the impact zone. Your aiming point technique not only will establish a forward swing bottom, but the point itself will help you align yourself correctly in the address position. When you locate it (with your peripheral vision) again at the top of your swing, it will snap into a clear focus the image of your straight plane line inscribed on the ground, which will guide you through your circular swing path (inside the straight plane line before impact, then inside it after impact) through the impact zone. Finally, a flat left wrist, again, a product of load, lag, and aiming point, will provide the physical structure you need to withstand the force of impact and keep your club swinging on-plane, through the impact zone.

Some readers may find it surprising that I have focused or limited my discussion of the swing plane to the impact zone. Ironically, most of the reading golfers have done about the swing plane has dealt with (rather obsessively, in my opinion) everything but the impact zone. However, the same rule of geometry that defines an on-plane swing through the impact zone applies to the entire golf swing as well, i.e., that the end of the club closest to the plane line at any point during the swing will always point at that plane line, and at any point during the swing in which the club shaft is parallel to the ground, it will also be parallel to the plane line.

Yet, I'll play devil's advocate and ask: if this were such an inviolable and sacred law of the swing, then why did Tiger Woods win the 1997 Masters tournament by twelve shots by taking his club slightly inside, or under, the "ideal" backswing plane, and also win the U.S. Open in 2000 by fifteen shots, with the club shaft either on or slightly above the backswing plane, then win the U.S. and British opens in 2005 with the club shaft noticeably above the plane on the backswing? The answer is that, however Tiger took the club back, he fully loaded his club, and then lagged it down, in relation to the straight plane line, through the impact zone, which is where it counts. In this regard, the old Scottish saying is completely correct: "You don't hit the ball with your backswing."

This book hopefully honors that wisdom and redirects golfers' attention to what is going on through the impact zone, meaning that they have swung their club on a straight plane line directed straight at their target.

I'm not saying that working on a technically on-plane backswing will hurt a golfer's game, but thinking that it alone will create a dynamic swing is like taking an aspirin to treat a very serious medical condition: It may help a little, but it doesn't sufficiently deal with the problem.

I can't tell you how many instructors I've witnessed who begin to work on a 30 handicapper's backswing plane, long before they work on their swing dynamics. No wonder so many golfers feel helpless. It's not that they are working on the wrong thing, it is more like their instructors have enrolled them in a course for a master's degree, when they haven't reached high school yet. Improving the swing's dynamics should supersede working on anything else, for both the accomplished and the beginning golfer alike.

I trust I've persuaded you that the club shaft must remain on-plane through the impact zone, in order to start the ball on-line with your target. Once you master the start line of the shot, all you have to control is how the ball curves. We'll talk about this later in the chapter. But you would have eliminated the critical variables of the start line and thus improve your consistency.

Let me tell you a story about how, during my days as a college golfer at BYU, I improved my fifth dynamic of swinging the club on a straight plane line through the impact zone. During the winter of my freshman year, Utah was blanketed with snow. I often made my way to the mountains for some snow skiing, but, in the evenings, I would return to campus and head to the Smith Fieldhouse. This fabulous indoor athletic facility had a 40-yard by 30-yard Astroturf sports practice area with a large canvas at one end. (I would have to practice swinging for at least ten minutes after skiing, before I even thought of hitting a golf ball, as those back and shoulder muscles would be pretty tight.) I asked my college golf coach, Karl Tucker, to place a vertical line down the canvas, which extended from the ceiling to the floor. Then I would set up 30 to 40 yards away from the canvas and hit long irons and fairway woods into the canvas, paying special attention to where the ball would strike the canvas in relation to the line, and I made whatever small adjustments I needed to get the ball to start on-line.

I would also continually monitor my setup and make sure that my eyes were tracking down my true target line, as this is a skill that must be learned and practiced independently (see "The Coin Drill," below). Invariably, I'd find that, if my eyes were tracking properly to the target, but I was still starting the ball to the left of the line, the problem was in my ball position. The farther forward the ball position, the farther to the left the ball started. Conversely, the farther back in my stance I played the ball, the more likely the ball flew to the right of the line on the canvas.

Once I verified that my ball position was correctly three inches inside my left heel (my own, personal best ball position mark), I would again hit shots, observing where, in relation to the line (or, of course, if the ball hit the line), the ball was striking the canvas. If the ball was still striking the canvas to the right of the line, this time I would work on clearing my left hip earlier and more strongly in my downswing (meaning, turning it to the left), while, of course, always making sure my swing dynamics were intact. This earlier clearing of the left hip would bring the ball back to the center line, in addition to increasing my club head speed—and that never hurts.

After weeks of this sort of practice, I had narrowed my range of shots that started off line. I was beaming with confidence and, once the snow thawed, I looked forward to seeing the result when hitting shots outside. Much to my amazement, though my shots started beautifully on-line as I expected, they also hooked terribly to the left. The shots simply didn't travel far enough indoors to reveal this hook. After pondering the problem, I figured out that the hook resulted from my overly strong grip, and that weakening it (by turning the left hand more to the left and the right hand positioned more on top of the grip) would solve the problem, which it instantly did. I went on to have the best spring and summer of my golfing life up to that point, winning two large college tournaments, five big amateur summer events, finishing as the low amateur in the U.S. Open, and becoming the number-one-ranked amateur golfer in the United States.

Keep in mind, however, that golfers must master the Fifth Dynamic before working on a grip change, because swinging the club shaft on-plane through the impact zone influences the initial direction of the ball's flight, while one's grip kicks in a second later, to determine the spin on the ball and curve characteristics of the shot. Too many people try to change their grip to change the curve of the ball, before mastering the straight plane line dynamic. This usually creates shots that do indeed fly straight, but straight off-line, to the right or to the left, in relation to the target line. It's far more effective to first work on starting the ball on-line, via the correct execution of the Fifth Dynamic, than to adjust your grip to correct hooks or slices.

Throughout the years, I have had fun inventing new ways to work on ways of improving my Fifth Dynamic. I have practiced trying to hit trunks of trees, telephone poles, and a fence post—or just about anything that sticks up vertically from the ground and is positioned along the initial line of flight of my shot. I still periodically stick an old shaft in the ground 5 yards in front of the ball on the range and challenge myself to hit the shaft. Of course, you need a low-lofted club for this drill, say a 2-iron or 3-wood. With more lofted clubs, the goal becomes starting the ball over the top of the shaft.

Not only did working on the Fifth Dynamic in college improve my ball striking, it also gave me a newfound confidence for escaping from the trees. Instead of just chipping back to the fairway from the woods, I began looking for more openings through the trouble that were in line with the green. I would often challenge myself to hit through narrow gaps in the trees, and I would make some great escapes.

In fact, golfers often notice that they hit their best drives on holes with the narrowest fairways, and their straightest iron shots when escaping from trouble. This is because these confining conditions force golfers to improve their alignment, and to swing their club along a straight plane line through the impact zone. Just think about how much straighter you will hit the ball when you execute the Fifth Dynamic successfully on each and every one of your golf shots!

I was not the only player on the PGA Tour who had fun working on their Fifth Dynamic. I can remember, in the mideighties, playing the final round of the Memorial Tournament in Dublin, Ohio, at the Muirfield Village Golf Club, where I was paired with the event's hosts, Jack Nicklaus and fellow tour player Greg Powers. There was a long rain delay, and when play finally resumed we all headed back to the ninth tee, where we had left the course. When I arrived, Greg was already on the back of the tee, hitting some old balls back into the woods. (That was allowed back then.) Greg was always looking for ways to make golf practice more fun, and sensing he was up to one of his tricks, I casually asked him, "What are you doing?"

"Do you see that V in that tree?" he said. "I'm trying to hit this drive through it. So far I'm zero for five."

Seeking a friendly challenge, I asked my caddy for a ball. I proceeded to go 0 for 5, as well. As I was finishing, up strolled Jack himself.

"What are you characters up to?" he asked in that high-pitched voice of his. I was first concerned that Jack might not think too kindly of our antics; after all, this was not only his tournament, but his course as well. But I went with the flow and said, "See that V in the tree Jack? We're trying to hit the ball through it."

"Angelo, give me a ball," Jack shouted to his caddie. His first shot went right through the middle. We all laughed! After we teed off, Jack began telling stories about his early years of trying to hit targets in front of him. He developed a drill of looking at a spot in front of the ball for better and more consistent alignment at address, and found that when he used the spot, he was more successful at starting the ball on-line. He would always monitor where the ball was starting, in relation to his target line. Does it surprise you that the greatest player ever employed the straight plane line dynamic without even knowing it? It doesn't surprise me in the least.

Jack had hit a perfect drive off that ninth tee, but then hit a fat short-iron shot into the water and made a double bogie, while Greg and I hit less-than-perfect drives, but made pars. Yes, even Jack Nicklaus is human.

When I was quite a bit younger, I also learned from Jack that a full understanding of the straight plane line dynamic allows you to draw the ball from left to right, or fade it from right to left.

Working the ball in either direction becomes a valuable tool that allows you to attack pins that are set on different parts of the green, to contour, or shape, your drives in harmony with dog-legged holes, or when you want to keep your ball away from trouble. You also need to learn how to work the ball to success-fully negotiate the wind. This was the gist of the lesson I learned from Jack.

It was 1977, and I was a seventeen-year-old kid playing in the U.S. Junior Championship, at Ohio State's Scarlet Course, in Columbus, Jack's hometown. Jack's son Jackie, who is my age, was also in the field and, since I had finished my morning round, I headed out in the afternoon to watch Jackie play. The truth is, beyond feeling thrilled to be playing on the same course Jack had competed on during his college career at Ohio State, I was hoping to meet the great man, as I knew he was at the event to watch his son play. Sure enough, I caught up with Jack on the third hole, introduced myself, and asked if I might walk with him for just a little bit. He said to come along, and what ensued was four hours in which I never left his side. We talked golf the whole day, which laid the foundation for a true friend-ship.

Jack's attention really perked up when the subject turned to Pebble Beach. He had said, and continues to say to this day, that if he had one round of golf left in his life to play, he'd tee it up at Pebble Beach. Of course, Pebble Beach had been another one of my team's home courses when I attended Robert Louis Steven-son High School (okay, we weren't the poster school for under-funded athletic programs!), so I felt we had settled on a subject about which I might have something to say, something that Jack would find interesting. In fact, Jack and I went through an entire virtual round of golf at Pebble Beach, shot by shot.

Of course, we discussed Pebble Beach's legendary windy conditions. After all, I had experienced them firsthand many times, which is to say there were calm days in which I hit a little sand wedge shot to the 107-yard, par-3 seventh hole, and days, with the wind off Carmel Bay howling fiercely in my face, when I had to drive a low-flying 4-iron to the green. When I played in the 2000 U.S. Open at Pebble Beach, the winds picked up on the seventh hole to the degree that I used a 7-iron.

Jack's wind lesson was direct and simple; after all, you don't become the greatest player of all time by overly complicating this already intricate and difficult game. Jack said you should work the ball back into the wind for accuracy, but you ride your ball with the wind for extra distance. People remember Jack's fabulous record, but I don't think they give him credit for being one of the greatest shot-makers ever.

In fact, Jack's method for working the ball in both directions struck the golf world as a bit odd, when he first began expressing it in his written instructional articles and in his book, *Golf My Way*. As you will see, Jack's way of intentionally curving the ball represents a slight variation of the Fifth Dynamic, the straight plane line.

In order to hit a fade, Jack simply rotated his straight plane line at address to the left of his target. He then aligned his club face directly toward his target, so that it appeared, and, indeed, was, slightly open to his new straight plane line. He could now take his normal swing and release the club, on-plane, and through the impact zone, in order to hit a shot that would start left of his target, then curve or fade back to it. We talked about playing this kind of controlled and accurate left-to-right flying fade on holes such as nine and ten at Pebble Beach, where the wind generally blows from right to left off the bay, and where trouble lurks down the right side of both holes.

When Jack wanted to hit a draw, to ride a right-to-left wind, either to ride the prevailing wind on the long number-two hole at

Pebble Beach, or off the famed eighteenth hole, where the pre-ferred shot is usually a draw off the tee (which, in this case, rep-resents working the ball for accuracy back into the wind, coming in from the left off the bay), he first established his straight plane line slightly to the right of where he wanted his ball to finish on the fairway. Then he addressed the ball with a closed club face, in relation to that new plane line, which still saw the club face aimed at his ultimate fairway landing area. By swinging along his new straight plane line, Jack's drive would start right of its destina-tion, then curve back to it, with a beautiful right-to-left flying draw that would ride the wind for extra distance.

It's worth pointing out that Jack was the first superstar I know of to teach working the ball this way, and it quickly caught on as the preferred method among pros and amateurs alike. Previously, the conventional method to do it required golfers to strengthen their grips (turn them to the right on the handle, for righties) and rotate their hands leftward aggressively through impact, to produce a draw, and weaken their grips and restrain their hands and wrists, and their forearm rotation, through the impact zone, to hit a fade.

Jack's (and my) method produces more consistent results be-cause of its simple and sound geometrical approach, one that the golfer can easily verify visually, right from the address posi-tion. The older way of working the ball invites inconsistency, be-cause of the difficulty of producing the desired amount of club face rotation (or restricting it, in the case of hitting a fade) on any given shot.

There is a nice little epilogue to this story that I recall with particular fondness: Later that year, I was playing in the National Insurance Youth Classic, up in Napa County, a good three hours north by car from Pebble Beach. Early Wednesday morning, I de-cided I wanted to watch Jack Nicklaus play a practice round at Pebble Beach, where he was competing in the 1977 PGA Cham-pionship (as it turned out, Lanny Wadkins, with whom I worked at CBS, won that championship). So a buddy of mine and I jumped in the car and made the drive south, in time to watch Jack warming up on the practice range.

There was a huge crowd, as usual, watching Jack hit balls, but that didn't stop him from turning around, spotting me among the throng with those penetrating and intelligent eyes of his, and saying, "Bobby, what are you doing here? Aren't you supposed to be up in Napa playing in the Big I?" In addition to being shocked and flattered that Jack noticed and spoke to me, I saw just how keenly tuned in to his environment he was from the moment he arrived on the golf course. It definitely made my day, and it made the six-hour round-trip from Napa well worthwhile.

As I said at the start of this chapter, the straight plane line dynamic is equally important in the short game. Golfers can have the great dynamics of a flat left wrist when putting, strike the ball with a good forward swing bottom when chipping (and pitching), load the club properly when pitching, but because of poor alignment left or right, continually miss their short shots' targets.

I often catch myself (and I observe others doing this as well) aiming too far to the left on pitch shots. Most of us have been taught to play pitch shots with an open stance. However, the feet alone don't account for true aim—the alignment of the shoulders is equally, if not more important; but the open stance can affect the way you track your eyes from the ball to the target and can cause you to aim left of the target. Again, aiming incorrectly can cause you to shift or bend your straight plane line, even during the quick interval of a short-shot swing, and doing so will break down your swing dynamics just as much as it will on a full-swing shot.

Even aiming slightly off-line becomes hazardous. When you look at the larger percentage on tour of made putts from three feet, compared to those made from eight feet, it's huge; and what could account for the discrepancy but faulty aim? One must set up at the target, and more importantly, swing on a straight plane line through the impact zone on putts, chip, pitch, and long shots equally. Making sure that you track your eyes correctly along your straight plane line, regardless of the positioning of your stance, will help you do so.

THE STRAIGHT PLANE LINE
DYNAMIC DRILLS

THE INTERMEDIATE TARGETS DRILL

Grab a 5-iron. (A 5-iron is a good middle-length club to practice with.) Place a coin five feet in front of the ball, in line with your target. Then stick a club shaft, or something similar, into the ground 10 yards in front of the ball, in line with the target. Practice lining up to the coin, then tracking your eyes to the shaft in the ground and then to the target. Practice this a few times, then hit the shot. Having someone stand behind you and tell you whether the ball started left or right of your target can provide helpful feedback.

If the ball is consistently starting to the left of the target, try moving it back in your stance a little bit. If you are still pulling the ball to the left, try visualizing your target more to the right, and aim your hands on the downswing more toward the inside part of the ball, so that you feel as if you are going to push the ball to the right of your target. Do this until the ball consistently starts on line.

If the ball is consistently starting to the right of the target, try moving it more forward in your stance. If you are still pushing the ball, work on clearing the left hip quicker on the down-swing, so that the hands will aim and swing more quickly and far-ther to the left through the impact zone.

If your shots start on your intended line of flight, but then hook or slice off line downrange, feel good about the fact that you have swung correctly on-plane through the impact zone, then make a grip adjustment. To correct hooks, weaken your grip by turning your hands to the left on the handle of the club. To correct slices, strengthen your grip by turning your hands to the right on the handle of the club.

The same drill can be used indoors, hitting into a net using a coin alone, without placing a shaft or other object in front of it. Simply place a coin five feet in front of your ball on your hitting mat and allow it to establish your straight plane line as you hit balls into the net.

THE PLUMB LINE DRILL

When I am really focusing on the Fifth Dynamic, and want to get my alignment precision-tuned, I head to the hardware store and pick up one of the carpenter's plumb lines. A plumb line is a tool used by builders, which uses string and chalk to create straight lines. It's a great ten-dollar tool for golf.

Golfers have most commonly used these plumb lines on the putting green to help improve putting alignment, but being able to draw straight chalk lines gives you a variety of opportunities to gain visual perspective on your alignment for full shots as well. The most important line is always the target line, which extends through the ball to the target. Additionally, drawing a series of parallel lines, say, along your heel line in relation to the target line, gives you a greater perspective on your overall alignment and aim.

After drawing these lines with the plumb line on the ground, you can step back into your address position and feel your whole body square, meaning, it is positioned parallel and perpendicular to your ball-to-target line. Don't get too caught up in making sure every muscle group is square to the target, but do get that "squared-up" feeling in relation to the ball, as if you were facing a wall. After you're comfortable that you've addressed the ball squarely, begin to trace your eyes, right eye under the left eye, down the target line and to the target. Repeat this many times out there on the practice range, even for fifteen minutes or more, before even striking a shot. Then begin to hit some shots, continually monitoring your setup and your visual alignments to your target.

Chalk lines drawn by the plumb line can also be used for

determining swing bottoms as well. To do so, simply draw two additional lines four inches apart, and perpendicular to your heel line and the ball-to-target line. Place the balls on the rearward line and set up to them in your normal square address position. Then begin striking shots, monitoring how your swing bottom relates to the forward line.

Picture 1: The shot started a hair to the right of the target. I made a small correction, moving the ball a half inch more forward in my stance. The result in picture 2 speaks for itself. It's perfect! Through constant use of this drill, I've improved my start line on my shots. The better your start line, the more accurate a player you'll become. *(Photos by Kerry Corcoran.)*

Hopefully, you've mastered the dynamics to the point of getting the swing bottom the magical four inches in front of the ball. What's more, pay attention to just how aligning yourself squarely actually *facilitates* achieving a swing bottom four inches in front of the ball. It does so because, in promoting all of your other swing dynamics (most pertinently, Dynamic Number Five, swinging along a straight plane line), it encourages an uncompensated swing, and an uncompensated swing always produces better swing dynamics.

BULLET POINTS

• If, in the putting chapter, I described a putt as a "miniature drive," it's logical to reverse the comparison and talk about a drive as a gigantic, or extended, putt. The point is, with every shot you hit in the game of golf, from a three-foot putt to a 300-yard drive, you want your club shaft pointing at the straight plane line through impact, along the intended line on which you want your shots to start. Golf may not be a game of "perfect," but it definitely is a game of "straight."

• Swinging on-plane simply means that the club head and shaft approach the ball from inside the straight plane line, while at the same time the club shaft points directly at it, from the instant the club head and shaft swing down past their parallel-to-the-ground alignment, until the moment the club makes contact with the golf ball. At that point, the club head and shaft actually touch the straight plane line for the first time since they did at address.

• When golfers throw away their lag prematurely from the top of the swing, they immediately lose their angle between their left arm and the club shaft. This leads to an overuse of the hands and wrists, which tosses the club off of its circular orbit, and more often than not redirects it from outside the target line, back across it to the inside. This changes the straight plane line by bending it to the left, and impact becomes a glancing blow that usually imparts a slicing left-to-right spin on the ball.

• Throughout the years, I have had fun inventing new ways to work on improving my Fifth Dynamic. I have practiced trying to hit trunks of trees, telephone poles, and a fence post, or just about anything that sticks up vertically from the ground and is positioned along the initial line of flight of my shot. Instead of just chipping back to the fairway from the woods, I began looking for more openings through the trouble in line with the green.

- A straight plane line qualifies as the Fifth Dynamic, simply because swinging in correct relation to it, through the impact zone, allows golfers to strike the ball with all of their other four dynamics completely intact and uncompromised.

CHAPTER SIX

THE IMPACT OF EQUIPMENT:

How Your Equipment Can Help or Hurt Your Swing Dynamics

Golf equipment today has reached a level of technological complexity never before imagined, for a game that basically boils down to hitting a ball with a stick. However, it might do golfers well to remember that, with all of the help one's gear can give them, they still have to execute a dynamically sound swing through the impact zone. As the great Sam Snead once quipped, "You can't buy a swing in the pro shop!"

That said, this chapter will look at your drivers, irons, sand wedge, and putter, in relation to the five swing dynamics, and look into how your equipment either complements or interferes with them. I'll also briefly touch on grips and the golf ball, to make sure that they, too, support a dynamic swing through the impact zone.

Golfers would do well to emulate their favorite tour players and take their equipment very seriously. Andy Brumer once interviewed my old pal David Ogrin, a former full-time tour player (and a past winner on the PGA Tour), and the topic turned to equipment. Responding to the question, "How important is your equipment to you?" David, never at a loss for an incisive reply to any question about golf, answered, "As important as a dentist's tools are to him or her." In other words, ouch! Playing golf with poorly suited equipment can really hurt!

If you still doubt the importance of equipment to today's best players, just stroll behind the driving range during a practice round at any tour event, and you'll see a parking lot full of huge equipment vans with the familiar names of Callaway, TaylorMade, Nike, Cleveland Golf, and PING (amongst others) printed on their sides. I can assure you they are not there to sell these tour stars a set of new clubs, but, rather, to respond to their every equipment whim and wish, whether it's adjusting the lies and lofts on their irons, reshafting their drivers, grinding a wedge, or lengthening or shortening a putter.

I saw John Daly in a recent episode of his Golf Channel TV show, "The Daly Planet," hitting balls at the TaylorMade test-and-fitting facility in Carlsbad, California. John asked that they flatten his new irons a bit, then, obviously pleased when they came back out of the plant for him to hit, muttered loud enough for the mike to hear, "It's amazing what a quarter of a degree flatter will do!" He ended the segment of the show with some advice to amateurs: "Get fit for your clubs; don't just buy them off the rack!"

Certainly, a lot is being said and written about club fitting in today's magazines, but nowhere do we really find a definition of exactly *what* is being fit. The answer is, that a golf club needs to "fit" (in this case, meaning to help facilitate) the production of the five swing dynamics of a flat left wrist at impact, a forward swing bottom, a club whose loaded power has been stored via lag, and delivered to and through the impact zone along a straight plane line. A person would never think of buying a pair of shoes into which their feet do not slip comfortably. Likewise, no golfer should buy or play with clubs that don't allow their swing to fill out their impact zone mold.

Sometimes you have to be a little adventurous when it comes to trying a new piece of golf equipment, or a new technology. Gary Player, for example, ever the innovator in all aspects of the game, won the 1965 U.S. Open with black fiberglass shafts in every club in his bag, including his putter, from a company called Shakespeare. These shafts were the precursors of today's graphite shafts, and Gary had the courage to use them when nobody else even knew what they were, solely because they improved his dynamics. Gary once told Andy Brumer in an interview, "I've always wanted to try out the newest technology, because I don't want to find myself sitting on a rocking chair on my porch one day, thinking, 'I should have given that club or that shaft or ball, or whatever it may be, a try.' " Of course, I find it hard to imagine Gary ever sitting on a rocking chair, idling away the day. It's just not in his makeup to do so.

I found myself very much in a Gary Player–like equipment situation back in 1981, shortly after the late Gary Adams introduced the first mass-marketed TaylorMade metalwoods to the golfing public. I had gotten off to a pretty good start in my career on tour, so, naturally, all the club-makers' reps wanted me to try their stuff. Having said that, my fellow pros and I were indeed a bit miffed when the TaylorMade rep handed us the first metalwoods to try. But try it out I did, and while it had a very different kind of feel and sound than did my persimmon driver and fairway woods, I found that, because of its low center of gravity, and even though it had a 1, presumably to signify a driver, stamped on its sole, I could really kill that thing off the fairway. In fact, I thought of the club more as a 2-wood than a driver.

Now, here's a bit of golf trivia that may impress your friends at your golf course's nineteenth hole: Who was the first golfer ever to be seen hitting a metalwood on television? That would be *me.*

It was 1981, I was competing in the Buick Open at Warwick Hills Golf and Country club, near Detroit, and I had the Taylor-Made metalwood in my bag. Each of the course's four par-5s were just out of my reach in two—until, that is, I went for them with this club, which got me either on the putting surface or just to the fringe.

I was vying for the lead, which meant the TV cameras had me well in their sights during the final round. I hit a long drive on the par-5 sixteenth hole, then pulled out the TaylorMade for the TV broadcast crew to see for the first time. Its silvery gleam understandably both caught their attention and caused some confusion for commentator Ben Wright, who was calling the action for CBS Sports.

"Well, it looks like a fairway wood, but it *isn't* wood," or something to that effect, is how Ben approached the subject of that club.

"Wait a minute, it's made of metal!" Ben exclaimed. "Why, I guess we'll have to call it a 'fairway metal,'" he concluded, and I'll be danged if the name didn't stick!

That club helped me get into a playoff for the title with Hale Irwin, Gil Morgan, and Peter Jacobsen, all great fairway wood players, by the way. Though I didn't win the event, these guys, and the rest of the golfing world, it turns out, paid pretty good attention to my club. From the following week on, TaylorMade metalwoods found their way into the bags of more and more tour players, and the rest, as the say, is history.

In the 1982 U.S. Open at Pebble Beach, where I finished third to Jack Nicklaus and the winner, Tom Watson, my "fairway metal" did indeed allow me to nearly reach the world's most famous par-5 eighteenth hole in two during the last round, which at that time represented a significant feat.

For you true golf trivia buffs, here's another tidbit of metalwood lore: Ron Streck, who now plays the Champions Tour, was the first player to use a TaylorMade metalwood in a PGA Tour event, the 1981 Byron Nelson, though he hand-painted the metal black, to look like a persimmon driver, because the club made him feel self-conscious. I must have been destined for the cameras, because even though Ron won the tournament—which was shortened to fifty-four holes because of rain—the cameras never bothered to set themselves on Ron at all during the entire event.

Now, I'm amazed to think that many of the game's best young players today, even some on the PGA Tour, may have never hit a persimmon driver or fairway wood in their lives! I hope, at least, that they've seen one! Of course, I'm now a CBS golf analyst myself, and, should I spot such a relic in the hands of a tour player today, I'm sure I'd be every bit as perplexed as Ben Wright was when he saw me pull out my TaylorMade metalwood back in 1981. Should that happen, I might even honor Ben's inventiveness by calling the thing a "woodmetal!"

Again, the point here is, the only reason to put a new club in your bag is if it helps you improve your swing dynamics.

I could spend days and days exploring the technical intricacies of today's golf clubs, but that's not the goal here. Rather, what I want to do is take a general look at the components of a golf club, i.e., the club head, shaft, and, briefly, the grip, and discuss them both individually and in conjunction with each other, as they ideally work in unison with your swing to produce dynamic impact.

THE CLUB HEAD

I'll begin with driver heads, and while many of them today clock in at the USGA's size limit of 460 ccs, it's often the small things about them that influence dynamic impact the most. Take the driver's loft, for example. Insufficient loft on drivers is one of the major swing-killers in golf, and before I go into why, it's important to point out that today's best golf balls are designed to deliver optimum distance and accuracy when launched at a high angle (from 11 to 13 degrees) and a spin rate of between 2,000 to 2,500 rpm (and up to 3,000 for players with slower club head speeds). Many club fitters, and even retail golf equipment shops, have sophisticated, computerized launch monitors with which golfers can test different clubs and select ones that produce the ideal driver-launch numbers. First off, since the definition of today's "perfect" drive is one launched high, with little spin, it makes no sense to play with a driver that doesn't have enough loft.

The problem is what's too little loft for one person's swing is the right amount of loft for another's. What, then, from the point of view of a dynamic swing, is the warning sign or symptom of a driver with an insufficient amount of loft for any given player? Assuming a golfer has the proper shaft in his or her driver, too little loft can result in the player hanging back on his or her back foot through the impact zone, in an attempt to swing up on the ball, so as to add the loft that's missing in the club head's design. Such a reverse pivot more often than not leads to a total breakdown of each of the five dynamics. This is an all too common problem that I see repeatedly when playing with amateur golfers. The problem starts when they get the club as a gift from someone, rather than going through the proper process of testing for a new one by hitting off a launch monitor.

Here's why people playing with insufficiently lofted drivers risk losing their swing dynamics: First, the rearward movement of the body's weight during a reverse-pivot downswing moves the low point of the swing arc back behind the ball. As you know, a rearward swing bottom generally features a cupped left wrist at impact, rather than the required flat one. So that's two dynamics that insufficient loft in a driver wipes out at once: a forward swing bottom and a flat left wrist at impact.

Next, with an insufficiently lofted driver, the golfer might not only hang back, but also flip the club with a broken-down left wrist, to add loft through the impact zone. There goes the lag—

because, as I have said repeatedly, once lag is thrown away during the downswing, it cannot be recovered or regained.

Now, loading the club well creates a powerful and confident feeling in golfers because they sense they have created all the power they need to lag the club into the ball at impact. Yet, when playing with a driver deficient in loft, this confidence quickly becomes confusion. The internal dialog goes something like this: "Why should I bother to load the club, if I know I have to throw that load away immediately in the downswing, to create more loft?"

As I said in the full swing chapter, this early casting away of the club from the top throws the club out of its normal orbit and across the straight plane line, so now we've violated the Fifth Dynamic as well.

However, in an ironic twist, a golfer testing an insufficiently lofted driver can actually cheat the launch monitor and produce ideal launch-condition numbers, precisely *by* swinging with

Having an insufficiently lofted driver can encourage a breakdown in swing dynamics, in an effort to add loft. Note how the left wrist has broken down at impact, the shaft has lost its forward lean, and the swing bottom is behind the ball. Having sufficient loft, or even slightly too much loft, can be a benefit in improving swing dynamics (see explanation below). *(Photo by Kerry Corcoran.)*

poor dynamics. In other words, they can successfully carry out the above set of compensations and, with a broken-down left wrist at impact and an out-to-in swing path (with its often accompanying open club face, which adds spin), increase their launch angle and spin rate. Since most launch monitors don't measure side spin (i.e., slices and hooks), a completely dynamic-less swing can look awfully good by this computer's numbers. So, be careful when working with a launch monitor, and the best way to do so is to insist that your club fitter is also a PGA teaching pro, capable of separating your bad swings from the inappropriate clubs that may be producing them.

What about a driver with too much loft? Obviously, the danger is that a player will hit the ball too high with too much spin, though such a club poses less of a threat to breaking down a golfer's swing dynamics than one with too little loft. In fact, a skilled golfer with a higher-than-ideally lofted driver will often bow or arch his or her left wrist forward through impact (the opposite of cupping it or having it break down) to purposely deloft the club, which is most often accomplished by standing closer to the ball at address. A stronger weight shift to the left side through the impact zone will produce a more forward swing bottom and reduce effective loft at impact. This is commonly called "trapping" the ball, and using a slightly higher-lofted driver accommodates this action.

The point of this discussion is that it's better to err on the side of more loft than less when choosing a driver. In fact, I've noticed a trend on tour today to switch to higher-lofted drivers.

Now, here's an interesting fact about today's driver head designs: Mostly all of them yield the best results (i.e., high launch and low spin) when they strike the ball slightly above the center of their club face. This causes the ball to push the top of the club head a little back, which adds some extra loft (called *dynamic loft*) to the club. Contacting the club face slightly above its center also reduces the shot's spin. This gives you an even more convincing reason to strike the drive with a slightly descending blow, because doing so makes it easier to contact the ball higher on the club face.

These behemoth club heads have spawned an interesting new item on the equipment scene, the superlong tee. While the conventional tee measures approximately 2 inches, today's stretch closer to, or even a bit over, 3 inches. This growth spurt isn't a matter of better tee nutrition: The longer tee obviously allows golfers to tee the ball very high, so they can more easily strike the ball high on the club face. Of course, as you improve in striking down on the ball with your driver, you will now be able to tee the ball lower and still hit solid drives.

Because driver heads are built with what is called "roll" (an arc in the face from the top of the head to the sole), striking the ball above the center also explains why a driver with 9 degrees of loft can create a launch angle of 11 degrees or more. Therefore, a player using a driver with 9 degrees of loft can create 12 degrees of launch angle on shots struck above the center of the club face, which should eliminate any anxiety golfers may have about swinging down on the ball with the driver.

Again, the higher the player hits the ball on the club face at impact, the higher the launch and lower the spin rate will be. This fact also serves golfers well when they miss-hit the ball more in the center of the clubface (this sounds strange, doesn't it, *miscontacting the ball in the center of the club face*, but you can't argue with progress!), because such impact still produces 9 or 10 degrees of launch, even if the spin rate goes up (which decreases distance because of air friction). Some equipment manufacturers are building drivers with a lower CG, which brings the ideal impact location lower on the club face and more in line with its center.

In the old days, good players would keep the ball down and into the wind by purposely hitting it with the lower part of the driver face. But most equipment manufacturers don't recommend this anymore. Instead, reducing spin rate is the more critical factor with today's new technology, when driving into the wind. I used to kick the grass on the tee and place the ball directly on the grass when driving the ball into the wind. Technology has certainly changed the game, so few players use this technique today.

Today, players tee the ball up to the same height, and they play the same high-flying, low-spinning drive, when playing into the wind or with no wind, though they may trap the ball a bit, to get a slightly lower launch angle when facing the wind. In other words, it's the relative absence of spin (and therefore, friction) that keeps the ball boring through the wind, regardless of its height, while, previously, we had to literally try to keep the ball low and *under* the wind.

The longer hitters, like Vijay Singh and John Daly, generally have very low-lofted drivers, usually around 6 or 7 degrees. The faster a golfer swings, the farther the ball potentially flies, and therefore, the lower the initial launch angle the golfer needs. Just so you equipment techies don't send me e-mails, it's worth noting that Vijay starts out with a high-lofted driver of about 10 degrees, then has his manufacturer open its club face several degrees, which effectively reduces the club's loft to about 7 degrees.

The point is, that many short-hitting amateurs should be using drivers with 12–14 degrees of loft. Manufacturers continue to build such drivers for women, who generally have slower club

head speeds than men, and it's a sign of progress that many club makers now have high-lofted driver models for all golfers, with slower swing speeds.

DRIVER SHAFTS

Graphite shafts have almost completely replaced steel shafts in today's drivers, as evidenced by the fact that Tiger Woods, a long-time steel shaft holdout, has switched over to graphite. The main reason for this is that graphite, being lighter than steel, can increase one's club head speed by an average of 2–5 mph. For every mph in club head speed increase, ball speed will increase about 1.5 times. For every mph increase in ball speed, the ball will fly about 2 yards farther. Therefore, a 5-mph increase in club head speed will give a golfer about 15 yards additional distance.

With the larger-headed drivers, players need longer tees. Tiger is using a 2 ½-inch tee in the photo on the left. Note how more than half of the ball is above the club face at address, but at impact the ball is just above the club face's center. Tiger works hard on his equipment, making sure that the launch angle and spin rate on his drives (high launch/low spin) match up to get maximum distance.

When Tiger hits an iron (photo at right), he makes contact at impact higher on the face than at address. He is able to do this because of his great dynamics, through impact, that result in a downward and forward strike and a good-sized divot. (Photos by Warren Keating. Used with the permission of the PGA Tour and CBS Sports.)

For years, tour players shied away from graphite shafts because they feared that the consistency of the graphite was not equal to that of steel. Since graphite is a woven fiber, players often felt that each shaft behaved significantly different than another, and that the fibers tended to loosen or change characteristics with time. At one point in my playing career, I was being paid three thousand dollars a week extra just to use my graphite driver; but I went back to steel, when the driver felt different after a few weeks of using it. However, today's graphite is much improved and has playing characteristics much closer to those of steel than ever before; and with Tiger now firmly in the graphite camp, steel-shafted drivers will no doubt go the way of the persimmon wooden drivers and wound balata golf balls. That is to say they will become things of the past.

When selecting a graphite shaft for your driver, it's important that you choose one with the proper flex, so it will work in conjunction with the club head. A good rule of thumb to go by—and it's a generality that has withstood the test of time—is that, the stronger you are and the faster you swing the club, the stiffer your shafts should be; whereas, less strong, slower-swinging players will do better with more flexible shafts.

Simply put, a shaft too stiff for a given golfer can have the same effect as an insufficiently lofted club head, because excessive stiffness in shafts also tends to make you hit the ball too low. In an attempt to add the loft back to the club that the ill-fitting shaft has reduced, the golfer might hang back on his or her right side, and, as with an insufficiently lofted club head, lose downswing lag by uncocking the left wrist too soon.

What about excessively flexible shafts for any given golfer? They can result in loss of directional control, both to the left and right. To compensate for this, golfers may start their swings well to the left of their target, then pull them back to the right (or vice versa) as they enter the impact zone, in a classic Dynamic Number Five, straight plane line violation. Finding a shaft flex that fits you correctly makes life a lot easier and golf a lot more fun.

A shaft's flexibility also impacts the dynamics of loading and lagging, because, at the start of the downswing, you want your change of direction to load (and stress) the club against the fore-finger pressure point at the base of your right forefinger. In order for the golfer to feel this loading dynamic, the shaft has to have a little bit of flex in it, i.e., it must not be too stiff. Not only is it more difficult to maintain the load, and therefore the lag, of an un-stressed shaft (because the stressed shaft, in bending back in-stantly, has some lag in it), but a shaft too stiff for a golfer to stress feels wooden or "boardy." This lack of feel often results in the loss of lag as well, because you can't lag something you can't feel.

Graphite shafts also come with either stiff or more flexible tip ends. This becomes an important consideration, because a flexi-ble, or soft-tipped, shaft adds spin to the ball at impact. Combin-ing such a shaft with a high-lofted driver head may produce too much spin on the ball, resulting in shots that balloon or shoot upward, rather than bore at a high but still flat-through trajectory through the air. Conversely, a stiff-tip shaft may not produce enough spin for a particular golfer (usually one with slower club head speed), and hit shots that fly too low. Again, this can lead to a compensating, reverse-pivot move, with its early lag throw-away, and other dynamic-destroying compensations, intended to add loft to the driver through the impact zone.

Last but not least, one needs to choose a properly weighted shaft for his or her driver, and one with the correct length as well. My advice is never swing a driver that is too heavy and/or too long to control, i.e., one that leads to the breakdown of your dynamics. Most new drivers on the shelves at pro shops measure forty-five inches, though many pros play with forty-four-and-a-half-inch drivers, as I do.

Today, graphite shafts range from approximately 50 grams, to those that come closer to a traditional steel shaft's weight of about 120 to 125 grams. Many pros like me use a standard steel iron shaft, measuring 120 grams or so in my irons, which establishes quite a weight discrepancy between one's graphite-shafted drivers and irons. This equates to a difference in feel and timing, as well, as you alternately hit shots with your drivers and irons. If one is not careful, this feel variance can result in broken-down dynamics, because we will naturally swing a lighter club faster than we will a heavier one.

Today, I use graphite shafts in my drivers and my 3-wood. Though I currently have the same gram shaft weight in each (95g), many tour pros are using very light driver shafts (65g), and slightly higher ones in their 3- and 5-woods (say, 10g increase in each club). Most players find that this progressive increase in weight, as the fairway woods get shorter, helps them to transition smoothly from these clubs into their heavier-shafted irons.

Iron Club Head Design

The first thing one notices about the design of many contemporary irons is that they hit the ball farther than irons ever did before. I understand this, as courses are also getting longer and longer, too, mainly as an expression of their owners' hopes of attracting a professional tournament with its long-hitting PGA Tour pros.

Allow me to pause for a moment before talking about iron design, to express my sentiments on this topic of today's superlong golf courses. I am not one who believes that making a golf course longer automatically improves it, even for tour pros. Players who hit the ball farther will always have an advantage, no matter the length of the course they play. For example, Harbour Town is one of the truly great short courses on the PGA Tour. Davis Love, one of the tour's longest hitters, has won this event an unprecedented five times. But the shorter hitters also have a chance on such a course, which I think makes the competition there more interesting and a fairer test.

One has to control the ball on this course, to navigate the

narrow fairways and shape shots into the small greens. Are these not important parts of the game anymore, factors that we should make an effort to preserve? Pebble Beach, Riviera, and Colonial are still great courses today, and none are exceptionally long. I would never trade one of those gems for the newly lengthened Torrey Pines South, or the new 7500+-yard Redstone Golf Club in Houston.

I am an announcer at the Masters, having covered "Amen Corner" (holes eleven and twelve) for the past dozen years. I love to broadcast the tournament, but I think it's a tragedy that they have gone to such an extreme to lengthen the course so much. If your name isn't Tiger Woods, Vijay Singh, Phil Mickelson, or some other bomber, you might as well stay home, especially if the course gets some significant rain. I know that I'm not the only one who feels this way. Jack Nicklaus and Arnold Palmer recently made comments about this as well. When you go and play the latest course I designed, the Payne Stewart Golf Club in Branson, Missouri, be sure to bring your ability to shape shots.

But now, back to irons.

The design dilemma the club makers face in designing irons for average golfers is that while many players want to hit the ball farther with these clubs, most struggle to hit the ball high enough with them, as well. As I said in my discussion about drivers, stronger (meaning less) loft and added height are at design odds with each other. For many years, irons makers have designed a significant amount of offset into their so-called "game-improvement clubs." An offset iron finds a bent hosel that positions the club head behind the shaft, which adds loft to the club at impact (I'll explain why momentarily), to help golfers hit the ball higher. Today, with lighter metals, such as aluminum alloys and composite materials, such as graphite, available for club construction, club makers not only still use offset, but also build deeper iron heads themselves (measured from the club face to the back of the club). The weight they saved by using light-weight materials allows them to add extra weight low on the club head, as well. Here's how these design features work to produce higher-flying iron shots:

As the golfer swings the club into the impact zone with an offset, rear-weighted iron, centrifugal force pushes the club head forward, in an attempt to align the club's (rearward) center of gravity with the shaft at impact. This adds "dynamic loft" (meaning more loft) to the club face at impact, which tilts back, as it rushes forward, just as the head of an oversized driver does (in our discussion above) when it strikes the ball high on its club face. The problem is this forward movement of the club head, however slight, can encourage a premature uncocking of the wrists, and a rearward, instead of a forward, swing bottom through the impact zone.

When you develop your iron swing around this kind of severe offset, rear-weighted set of irons, look out for what happens when you pick up your driver and fairway woods. Too many amateurs have asked me to solve their problem, which is playing pretty well with the irons, but poorly with drivers and fairway woods. When I look in their bags and see these game-improvement irons, I shake my head and understand the source of their problem.

Yet, I'm really not making a total indictment of the game-improvement irons. Here's how I look it: If you are a player who is just beginning to work on swing dynamics, you may very well need help from the club to get the ball into the air, until your dynamics improve to the extent that you can trust them to do the job for you. Once a player's swing dynamics begin to improve, they should think seriously about moving into a blade iron design (that is, no cavity in the back at all), or at least a cavity-backed blade iron (meaning an iron with a partial, not a full, cavity). Here's why: Traditional blades feature a high center of gravity and much less offset hosels than their game-improvement counterparts (I'm just about old enough to remember a time when manufacturers made blades with no offset at all, and some still do.) Such clubs require golfers to strike pronouncedly down and through the ball, in order to contact it high on the club face to produce shots with sufficient height. While game-improvement irons, with their low centers of gravity, do doctor-up impact and provide acceptable results on shots struck low on the club face, blade irons simply will not. That is why they have come to take on an almost feared aura, and a knee-jerk reaction by a golfer that says, "I'm not good enough to play blades."

My writing partner, Andy Brumer, feels that these game-improvement irons trade the swing for the hit, because such irons can yield decent shots with undynamic swings. However, if you are ultimately concerned with improving your swing and not masking flaws, once you consistently achieve a swing bottom of two inches forward of the ball with your game-improvement irons, I suggest moving toward a blade-type design. Again, such clubs will both encourage and reward an aggressive move through the impact zone, and your swing bottom will begin to move toward that coveted four inches in front of the ball mark. This is why noted golf teacher Chuck Hogan has called blade irons *true* "game-improvement clubs." When this starts to happen, you'll start to see your driver and fairway-wood swings improve as well. Look at the photo on page 159 of Tiger's club head just after impact with an iron, and observe how high on the club face he strikes the ball.

Finally, remember that the so-called average golfer did just fine with blades prior to offset, game-improvement irons' arrival on the golf scene. In fact, have all of these game-improvement features on clubs resulted in the lowering of golfers' average handicaps? Statistics from the National Golf Foundation say no. Need I say more?

FITTING FOR LIE ANGLE ON IRONS

Equipment experts agree that it's absolutely essential for golfers to play with irons whose lie angles fit them properly. Simply put, an iron's lie angle refers to the angle formed between the club head and the shaft. Golfers who play with irons that are too upright for them will tend to hit shots off line and to the left, while those playing with irons that are too flat tend to lose shots to the right.

Here's why: An iron that is too upright for a given golfer strikes the ball with the toe too far up in the air. The heel of such a poorly fitted club catches and digs into the turf first, which causes the toe to close aggressively through the impact zone. This clockwise rotation of the club head imparts a right-to-left hook spin. The opposite takes place with irons that are too flat for a golfer. Now, the toe catches and digs first, which results in the heel passing through the impact zone before the toe. This opens the club face and produces slice spin and/or shots hit off line to the right (for right-handed golfers, of course). Another theory posits that irons that are too upright have an axis tilted to the left, and, in those that are too flat, one that tilts to the right. Therefore, these club faces point to the left or right respectively and cause off-line hits in both directions. While those in the know disagree over which theory is correct, they do concur that, in practice, overly upright irons, for any given golfer, cause shots lost to the left (for right-handed players), and those too flat cause shots lost to the right.

The good news is that the more forward you move your swing bottom via good swing dynamics, the less of a factor an improper lie angle will have on the shot. The reason is, the more forward the bottom of the swing, the deeper the club head penetrates into the ground—therefore, the less influence the ground will have on catching the toe or heel of the club and turning the club face during impact. One can also say the same the same for side-of-hill lies. Again, the more forward the swing bottom, the less effect the slope or hillside lie will have on the shot. Needless to say, I'm not recommending playing with poorly fitted iron lie angles, I'm only pointing out that a sound dynamic swing mitigates incorrectly fit clubs to some degree.

When an overly upright lie angle causes a player to consistently lose shots to the left, he or she will begin to compensate by unconsciously aligning, aiming, and swinging more and more to the right. The opposite, of course, is true for shots missed regularly to the right, due to overly flat irons: Now the golfer tends to aim and swing too far to the left. In both cases, the golfer aims in one direction and swings in another, and therefore clearly violates the Fifth Dynamic, of swinging along a straight plane line through the impact zone.

Keep this inherently complex game as simple as you can, by getting fit for a set of irons built to your proper lie-angle specifications. This will protect you from developing subconscious alignment problems, which can erode your swing dynamics faster than you might want to know.

THOUGHTS ON DYNAMIC PUTTER AND WEDGE FITTING

One can get very technical and involved with putter and wedge fitting, but I want to limit the discussion about these clubs to a couple of things. First, I think it's absolutely essential that the golfer have enough loft on his or her putter to elevate the ball out of the depression in which it sits when on the green, because this insures that the ball will roll smoothly to the cup. Standard putters have about 4 degrees of loft.

Putts that hop or bounce immediately after impact often point to an insufficiently lofted putter. The proper amount of loft also facilitates solid contact, because it allows the entire surface of the putter face to strike the ball; whereas a putter without enough loft tends to contact the ball obliquely, on the top portion of the club face. Such a putt will tend to skid and bounce as well, rather than roll smoothly. But how does loft affect dynamics?

In the first chapter (Dynamic Number One) we learned that a flat left wrist, both at impact and throughout the putting stroke, means that the left wrist and the club head move at the same rate of speed throughout the stroke. What happens when the golfer uses a putter without enough loft on it? In an attempt to add loft at impact, the golfer will invariably cup, or break down, his or her left wrist—which tilts the club face back and adds loft to the shot. It also means that the left arm and the putter swing at two rates of speed, which makes distance- and direction-control erratic at best. Golfers can eliminate or reduce this problem considerably, simply by making sure they have a putter fitted with sufficient loft.

Another common mistake golfers make when using a putter with too little loft is they move the ball placement too far forward in their stance, in an attempt to swing up on the ball, to increase loft. Most golfers also swing the putter on some type of arc, with the putter face opening slightly on the backswing, and then closing a bit on the downswing. As they move the ball forward in their stance, they may notice a better roll on the ball, but they also immediately will begin pulling their putts. Again, they will try to compensate for this by opening the club face even more through the impact zone, which will lead to even more erratic lines and inconsistent speed (i.e., more missed putts). I have found that I roll the ball best with a putter with between 4 and 5 degrees of loft.

Putting style can dictate the best amount of loft a golfer needs on his or her putter. Dave Stockton, one of the game's best putters, strikes decisively down on the ball, with his hands well forward at impact. Such a stroke delofts the putter face considerably, which is why Dave, and those who putt like him, use and need putters with slightly more loft on them. Your teaching pro, observing your stroke, can tell you how much loft you need on your putter, and a good repair shop can adjust your club accordingly (or you can custom-order your putter, with a specified amount of loft on it, from many of the top putter manufacturers).

You also have to pay attention to the length and lie angle of your putters, as both can affect your ability to swing the putter along a straight plane line.

A putter that is too long for a given golfer will position the left wrist in a more bent address position, which usually leads to a broken-down left wrist position at impact. Shorter putters can alleviate this problem (length, of course, is a relative variable, because a thirty-five-inch putter may feel long to a golfer five foot six, and short to one six foot five). I use a thirty-four-inch putter. Andy North and George Archer were both great putt-makers who used very short putters, despite being tall. They both putted with a very flat left-wrist address position and maintained this alignment throughout their putting stroke, just as I've recommended to you in chapter one.

Champions tour player Isao Aoki was (and still is) a brilliant putter, and his club has a lie angle that is very upright, in an exaggerated way (you can really see the toe of his putter point up in the air at address and impact). He purposely bends the lie angle of his putter this way, to ensure that it contacts the ball above its equator, which imparts overspin, rather than backspin on the ball, for a better roll. This is more of an old-style solution, as contemporary technology can improve the initial roll of the ball off the putter face and reduce the putt's skid.

For example, Yes!, the makers of the C-Groove putter line (and, again, a company that I professionally endorse), builds concentric grooves into their putter faces, which were designed to reduce the ball's skidding. It singlehandedly turned around Retief Goosen's career, when he switched to the putter two weeks before winning his first U.S. Open, in 2001.

SAND WEDGES

When selecting a sand wedge, it is important to match the degrees of bounce on the club (meaning the size of the angle from the raised flange on the bottom of the club to the ground) to your personal style of wedge swing. Bounce angles on typical

sand wedges range from 6 to 12 degrees. A 56-degree wedge generally has considerably more bounce on it than a 60-degree wedge. More bounce generally works better for a wide range of sand conditions, while wedges with less bounce work more effectively when hitting shots off firm sand and/or firm ground.

Golfers tend to fall into two categories of wedge players: those who swing steeply and dig deeply down and through the ball, and players who take a shallower, more sweeping divot. The "digger" can benefit with more bounce built into his or her wedges, because the trailing edge, or flange, will glide off of the turf, rather than the leading edge of the wedge digging into it. The more shallow striker might choose a wedge with less bounce, because one with a high flange (i.e., more bounce) might easily skid off the ground, then belly or blade the shot right in the middle of the ball and send it scurrying over the green, especially on shots played from firm ground.

Playing a wedge shot with the ball positioned back in the stance steepens the swing's angle of attack into the ball, and thus reduces the bounce of the club. Knowing this can be helpful when playing a variety of shots around the green. Often, when playing in the summer on the PGA Tour, players find themselves faced with hitting shots from around the green off trampled-down turf, thanks to the gallery. Since the PGA Tour already likes

With the club face more open, bounce is increased—which helps the sand wedge to go smoothly through the ball and create that sand "splash" we all like. *(Photos by Warren Keating. Used with the permission of the PGA Tour and CBS Sports.)*

to make their tournament courses play firmly, the ground underneath this trampled-down turf becomes like cement. These types of shots are best played with wedges that have as little bounce as possible, to reduce the possibility of blading the ball. That is why you will often see more experienced players positioning the ball back in their stance, when hitting these wedge shots.

When playing lob shots, or playing from a bunker, keep in mind that opening up the blade at address not only adds loft, but

also adds bounce. Bounce is most needed when playing out of soft sand, as the bounce keeps the wedge from digging into the sand as it goes through impact. As I've said, wet and heavy sand tends to also play firmly, and doesn't require as much bounce angle to play an effective bunker shot.

I set up my two sand wedges as follows: My 55-degree wedge has 12 degrees of bounce and my 60-degree wedge has 6 degrees of bounce. I hit a majority of my bunker shots with my 55-degree wedge.

From a dynamics point of view, a golfer who attacks his or her wedge shots steeply, but plays them with too little bounce on the wedge, may tend to unconsciously lose load and lag on the downswing (which, as we've said over and over again, collapses the flat left wrist at impact), in order to swing up on the ball and avoid sticking the club in the ground. It's among the sad cruelties of golf, that such a scenario tends to produce the completely opposite result, i.e., a thrown-away club head, dumped too far behind the ball and into the ground.

Conversely, the player who swings on a shallower arc through

Pages 171–172: With experience and the help of a PGA professional you can find the ball that compresses right for you. *(Photos by Warren Keating. Used with the permission of the PGA Tour and CBS Sports.)*

the impact zone, but uses a wedge with too much bounce on it, may also throw away his or her lag and flat left wrist, in an unconscious effort to deliver the club sharply under the ball, so as to prevent their wedge from skidding up into the ball's midsection.

GRIPS AND BALLS

I've given you a lot to think about in terms of equipment's impact on your dynamics, but I want to conclude with one thought each about grips and golf balls. Be sure to play with grips that fit your hands correctly, because excessively thick grips can make it difficult to set and load the club fully, and overly thin grips can result in overly active hands and early lag throw-away.

As for golf balls, play with those with the appropriate hardness for your swing speed. Today's tour-type balls require club head speeds of at least 100 mph (with a driver) to yield their full performance benefits. Players with slower swing speeds will find it difficult to compress such balls, and they will tend to hit them too low. They will try (either consciously or unconsciously) to add height to their shots, at a great cost to their dynamics, by hanging back during their downswing, throwing their lag away early, and cupping their left wrist, instead of keeping it flat through the impact zone. Balls too soft for faster swingers will spin excessively and fly too high, which can inhibit players from making an aggressive and dynamically sound swing through the impact zone.

The good news is that there are many golf balls on the market that offer different launch characteristics that are just right for a range of swings. Let your local PGA pro help you pick the ball that best compliments your swing and game.

BULLET POINTS

- Golfers would do well to emulate their favorite tour players and take their equipment very seriously. During an interview with my old pal David Ogrin, a former full-time tour player (and a past winner on the PGA Tour), the topic turned to equipment. David said that "Equipment is as important to a tour player as a dentist's tools are to him or her." In other words, playing golf with poorly suited equipment can really hurt!

- Assuming a golfer has the proper shaft on his or her driver, too little loft can result in the player hanging back on the back foot through the impact zone, in an attempt to swing up on the ball to add the loft that's missing in the club head's design. Such a reverse pivot more often than not leads to a total breakdown of each of the five dynamics. The problem starts when a golfer gets a driver as a gift from someone, rather than going through the proper process of testing for a new one by hitting off a launch monitor.

- Keep this inherently complex game as simple as you can, by getting fit for set of irons built to your proper lie-angle specifications. This will protect you from developing subconscious alignment problems, which can erode your swing dynamics faster than you might want to know.

- Putting style can dictate the best amount of loft a golfer needs on his or her putter. Dave Stockton, one of the game's best putters, strikes decisively down on the ball, with his hands well forward at impact. Such a stroke delofts the putter face considerably, which is why Dave and those who putt like him use and need putters with slightly more loft on them.

T

- Golfers tend to fall into two categories of wedge players: those who swing steeply and dig deeply down and through the ball, and players who take a shallower, more sweeping divot. The "digger" can benefit with more bounce on the wedges, because the trailing edge, or flange, will glide off the turf, rather than the leading edge of the wedge digging into it. The more shallow striker might choose a wedge with less bounce, because one with a high flange (i.e., more bounce) might easily skid off the ground belly, or blade the shot right in the middle of the ball.

CHAPTER SEVEN

MENTAL DYNAMICS:

Visualizing the Golf Swing Through the Impact Zone

People often say to me, "Bobby, it's great to learn the swing's dynamics, but how do I do it? How do I make a dynamic swing?" I talked at length, in each chapter, about how to mechanically execute the dynamics, so, by now the seeds of these dynamic images are well planted in your mind. Allow them to flower and grow there by thinking about and mulling them over, so to speak, even when you are not practicing them. Ultimately, though, you need to go beyond "head knowledge" and apply what you imaginatively see in your mind to actual, dynamic golf swings, out there on the golf course. This chapter will help you do so.

It helps to watch tour pros live or on TV, because their swings put the dynamics to work better than anyone's. There's a bit of the child left in all of us, therefore we all have retained an ability to emulate or mimic the swings we see and imprint them into our memory bank. Study your favorite tour pros' swings and picture yourself making those dynamic motions yourself.

You may be surprised to learn that Phil Mickelson's father started his son in golf left-handed, so that, when Phil faced his dad and watched him swing right-handed, he could easily mirror and imitate that swing.

You may be even more surprised to hear that many, if not most, tour players often watch their fellow competitors' swings and use them as models, as well. After all, theirs is a profession where any opportunity for an advantage needs to be grasped, as it can make the difference between winning and losing. Sure, during a tournament round, you may see golfers turn away from their playing partners' swings, because they want to fully focus on their own games, but during practice rounds they often keenly watch their fellow pros, hoping to pick up something that will help their own swings.

Chris Couch, who was at the point of almost quitting golf in 2004, wisely sat down with his former teammate at the University of Florida, Paul Tesori, who is Vijay Singh's caddie and part-time swing coach, to take an extensive look at videos of top players' swings. Chris used video to get a clearer picture of his own swing, and to create a mental image of his swing looking like that of the best players. Paul has taken much video of many top players' swings. Vijay himself often uses the video to take a look at his swing, as well as at the swings of other great players. All the tour pros know the value of getting a mental picture of how they want their swing to look.

I know that when my transition starts getting quick, which prevents me from fully loading and lagging the club (Dynamics Two and Three), I try to get a mental picture of Ernie Els or David Toms, both of whom have wonderful transitions. If I'm trying to get more swing speed, I might use Tiger Woods as a visual image. Or, if I want more lag on my downswing, I might picture Sergio

Garcia or Lucas Glover. If your visual image of the dynamic you're trying to improve is not firmly established in your mind, watching a top player live, on TV, or on video, can be a tremendous help.

There's scientific research that supports this strategy. For example, neurologists know that when a person imagines a physical activity (such as executing the five dynamics of a golf swing), the same region of their brain "lights up," to use the neurologists' own vernacular term, as if it were performing the action itself. So there is more than folk wisdom to the aphorism, "If you can imagine or dream it, you can do it." It has just taken modern science some time to understand what common wisdom has known all along!

In fact, I remember hearing interviews with Tiger when he was still a teenager, in which he said he developed his own technique by taking the best parts of the game's greatest swings and blending them into his own. That's your goal now as well: to integrate the swing's separate dynamic motions and images into a unified swing motion, which you can apply in actual golf shots on the course, even during a pressure-packed golf tournament.

Form a clear image of the dynamics, not only by observing the pros execute them, but by watching your teacher demonstrate them, as well. Study your progress by watching video of your own swing, and by imagining a swing with sound dynamics, when you're away from the course. However you do it, your mind will act as the glue that ties your swing's five dynamics together. Remember that your swing is always in a state of evolution. Like relationships, the only thing that's constant in the golf swing is change. Tiger Woods's oft-repeated message that he always strives to get better acknowledges this fact and expresses his ongoing commitment to integrating his swing changes into an even more dynamic motion.

Remember, it's important that you do not rush the process of improving your dynamics-guided swing. We live in a society that craves instant gratification and would have us believe that, after reading an instruction article in a golf magazine, by instant osmosis, the information programs the body to execute that lesson perfectly. But in golf you need patience and discipline in order to first absorb, understand, and imagine the correct swing dynamics, before upgrading them through practice and applying them in actual play.

I heard a little story from Brian Leroy, an attorney from Calgary, Canada, and a long-time golf student of my childhood teacher Ben Doyle, that reinforces this conviction: Brian and his wife Karen travel south each year to take lessons with Ben at his teaching location at Quail Lodge, in Carmel Valley, California, where I grew up. After one promising lesson, Brian confidently told Ben, "I really understand what you taught me today."

Ben, with his inimitable blend of authority and kindness, answered softly, "No you don't. You have knowledge. If you understood it, you could apply it."

In other words, it's really important that you fight your "I want it now" world, and realize that we all acquire skills gradually, through practice. I remember seeing a sign on the wall next to the office of a very clever and wise teaching pro. It said, "Series of ten golf lessons, $500; one golf lesson, $1,500. If you want a miracle, you will have to pay for it!" While the mind naturally enjoys synthesizing information and experience, and piecing parts into wholes, it does so at a different pace for each person.

Let me take this line of thinking one step further, and follow it along a slightly different, though very much related path. We often hear so-called teaching experts talk about the difference between "mechanics and feel." They'll tell you Freddie Couples or John Daly are "feel" players, and Nick Faldo and Bob Estes are "mechanical" types of players. I ought to know. People have been accusing me of being a mechanical player for as long as I can remember. Well, (how do the kids say it these days?) *Hello!* I've got news for you all: *All* tour players are feel players, period. They have learned their "mechanics" so thoroughly that there's really nothing left for them to do *but* feel them! Maintaining this dichotomy between mechanical and feel players, next to the misguided emphasis placed on swing style, rather than swing dynamics, is one of the most ignorant ideas too many well-meaning golf teachers continue to propagate today! This said, it's true that some tour players choose to integrate new mechanics into their swings more often than do others. But all great players succeed in translating these mechanics into their own feel.

In other words, it's one thing to talk about feel, but the larger point is, you want to feel the correct dynamics, not just any random swing movement that, by luck, happens to produce a good golf shot. The missing link in this equation, as I said above, is that it takes some time before a golfer can make this transition from proper mechanics to a subjective feel—and one has to start with mechanics first. Learn to execute your dynamics first, even if you miss the ball (an extreme example), and, gradually, you will see that as your dynamic motion improves, so will your shots. I promise!

I've heard it said that Pele, the great soccer player, once addressed a group of young soccer players and told them that it takes a thousand tries to learn a new move and ten thousand tries to perfect it. Soccer must be a harder game than golf, because I don't think you'll need that many swings to see your dynamics improve.

However, having said that, don't become discouraged if you find, at first, that your effort to apply one of the five dynamics feels awkward, different, or strange. In fact, *this is a good sign,* because it indicates that you are not swinging in your old way. I'd be more concerned if you do not feel a difference from your old swing at all, when you're beginning to work on these dynamics. So, again, be patient with them, and work on them from a mechanics starting point, until you can execute them by feel alone.

Pay close attention to that "Aha!" moment, when you begin to really feel your dynamics subjectively in your body. Then you can say "I'm a feel player," just like all of the pros. Remember, though, people will cross this bridge from mechanics to feel at their own pace and in their own good time.

This chapter offers some thoughts and guidance on the mental side of learning, understanding, practicing, and applying the book's five swing dynamics. In so doing, it also serves as a review of the entire book, whose very premise all along has been one of shifting your mental conception of the golf swing from one of style to one of dynamics, and of seeing golf through a whole new set of eyes.

Now, when you watch tour events on TV or in person, you will find yourself paying attention to the dynamic quality of these great players' swings. Instead of looking to see if a player started his or her swing to the inside or the outside of the ball, you'll observe the manner in which that player loads the club, and how he or she stores that load by lagging it through the impact zone. You may even find yourself peeking your head over the ropes to see if a player's bottom of the divot, on an iron shot, does indeed extend four inches in front of the ball. Rather than only waiting to see if a golfer holed or missed a putt, you'll notice how the better putters stroke the ball with their left arm, wrist and putter moving at the same pace, and how that insures a flat left wrist at impact and a solid strike.

When you go to take a golf lesson, or when you search for a new teacher, you'll have a much clearer goal as to what you want to accomplish with your instruction. It has become a common practice these days for golf pros to ask their students what goals they have, before beginning a series of lessons. I can just imagine the look of surprise on a teacher's face when you say, "I want you to help me work on and improve my five swing dynamics!"

From now on, when you read an instructional article in a magazine, rather than finding yourself confused and wondering how this generalized information applies to your specific swing, you will have the ability to discover the dynamic essence of the instruction, which will truly make it more useful to you. For example, let's say you read an article about "shifting your weight to your left side at the finish of your swing." Certainly, that looks great for the camera, but what about its dynamic value and meaning? As you've seen in the full swing chapter, shifting the weight forward through the impact zone assists you in sustaining your loaded lag, so that you can produce a forward swing bottom, with the center of your divot four inches ahead of the ball.

The key to taking your mental dynamics from the sports psychologist's couch to the golf course is learning to become process-oriented, and even this takes practice. Whether you're playing well, and the putts are all dropping, or you find yourself struggling with your game, you practice removing yourself from the larger context of your round and its score, and you narrow your focus on playing the game one shot at a time, every one to the best of your ability. When you feel that nervousness coming on, take some deep breaths, make a few more practice swings, steady yourself, and then execute.

What I'm really talking about is mental discipline, and the best way to learn this is by putting yourself in competitive situations over and over again. Everybody who wants to play competitive golf has got to keep striving for the next rung up the competitive ladder. That may start with a five-dollar Nassau with your buddies on the weekend, then move to local amateur tournaments, statewide tournaments, national tournaments, college golf, professional mini-tours, whatever. You're always trying to get to the next level of competition and to push yourself, because that's how you learn to play your best.

But, what about the recreational golfer who is never going to play in an actual tournament, or even in his or her club championship? A lot of people don't want to compete in golf, and that's fine. But they still want to improve their games, and I honestly think that, for the purpose of improving your game, competition is a necessary factor—even if you are playing by yourself and you are trying to beat your lowest score. That's a form of competition. Ultimately, golf is a game against the course and against yourself.

Now no matter how well we focus, how intent we are on executing, golf has a funny knack of thwarting the best of our intentions. I learned this lesson right out of the gate, so to speak, on one of golf's grandest stages.

It was the 1978 U.S. Open, at Cherry Hills Country Club in Denver, Colorado, and the first professional tournament I ever played in, though I qualified and participated in the tournament as an amateur. I was just past my eighteenth birthday, and, though all of one hundred and forty pounds sopping wet, I found myself in second place after the first round and in fifth place after the second. For the third round, I found myself paired with Lee Trevino, the former U.S. Open champion, and I was really caught up in the excitement of the moment. Jim McKay, the wonderful broadcaster, was there as the roving reporter for ABC Sports, and he was a favorite of mine as I grew up, watching and listening to him broadcast golf. When the U.S. Open came around each year, Jim raised his game a notch, as well, which didn't do much to settle my nerves when he approached me to say hello before my round with Trevino. What's more, I had hardly slept the night before and couldn't eat much for breakfast or lunch before my afternoon tee time with Lee. Of course, the fact that I looked so young that the locker-room attendants didn't want to let me in earlier in the week (caddies aren't allowed in the locker room!) didn't help matters, in terms of bolstering my confidence and making me feel like I belonged. In short, it was just a very, very difficult day for me, as thrilled as I was to be there.

My self-talk strategy for calming myself down went something like this:"Trust your swing and don't worry about what happens. Just do the best you can."

That's exactly what I had every intention of doing, when Lee and I stepped onto that first tee of the famous, short par-4 hole, whose green Arnold Palmer drove to, en route to winning the 1962 U.S. Open. (By the way, if you ever see the film clip of that drive, observe the small divot Arnold took with his driver, indicating a downward strike and a forward swing bottom, even with the driver!) Lee had the honor, and he took out a 1-iron. You may recall Lee's famous line, "Even God can't hit a 1-iron." (Sit tight, as I think we may have uncovered its genesis!)

We were playing into the wind, and there were thousands and thousands of people, maybe fifteen deep, in rows that lined that elevated tee box and first fairway. Needless to say, they formed a very narrow slot to hit through, and I had never come close to hitting a shot in front of that many people. When added to the facts that I was near the lead of our national championship, and was playing with the great Lee Trevino, this instantly raised my nervousness to a stomach-churning level. I was text-book fodder for any sports psychologist interested in doing a case study on performance anxiety.

Lee got up and was introduced. . . .

"The 1968 U.S. Open Champion, Lee Trevino!"

Of course, the crowd went wild—"Go get'm, Mex!"—that sort of thing. So what did he do? He completely topped the ball with that 1-iron. Completely topped it! The ball didn't even get up to the ladies' tee. It just dribbled off the front of the tee box. Now we know where the expression, "Even God can't hit a 1-iron," comes from!

Everyone just stood there shocked, perhaps me more than any of them.

I somehow managed to get my own 1-iron shot airborne and pulled it into the left rough. Lee took three more shots to get on the green. He was on in four, and took two putts for a double bogie.

I was just off the edge of the green with my second shot, and I had one of those lies in the deep grass at the edge of the green, which didn't faze me, because I'd been really proficient with that shot all week. My practice round partners, Billy Casper and Johnny Miller, had coached me on playing it as I would a sand shot, which involved opening my sand wedge and hitting behind the ball. In other words, I had this shot!

So, I got up there and I looked at the lie, determined my line, opened my sand wedge's blade, and made the same big swing I had practiced all week, to get the club through the grass. Then I looked up, expecting to see the ball tracking toward the hole. I looked up and . . . I *didn't* see the ball! So, I looked back down—and the ball was still at my feet! The ball had sat suspended in air, in the middle of the thick tall grass, and I had whiffed and missed the ball by swinging the club completely under it.

There I was, my first time on national television, playing with Lee Trevino, and I had just whiffed! I actually felt myself shaking, and thinking "How could this happen?" I had never in my life whiffed a ball before!

I composed myself the best I could, and went ahead and hit the shot again—*and I did the same thing!* A cold whiff again. Right underneath it. But the good news was that I had taken out enough grass with my two swings, so the ball was actually resting on the ground, and, with that better lie, I was able to pop my fifth shot up to about two feet from the cup, and I made the putt for a six, tying Lee.

As we were walking off the green, Lee turned, looked over at me, and said, "God almighty, man, can we start over?"

Of course, everybody started laughing, including myself. Sometimes you need a little comic relief like this, just to keep the game in perspective. I ended up shooting an 80 that day, and Lee a 75. However, while two whiffs in a row shook my composure, I did manage to focus, and I got myself process-oriented again during the final round, and ended up finishing thirtieth in the tournament, with an 80. I thought that was pretty good.

As I said earlier in this chapter, one of the best ways to improve your game is to play with golfers better than you. Now, we PGA Tour pros have pretty healthy egos, so it's not often that one will admit that their playing partner is "better" than he. However, the implicit sentiment on tour, I think, is that, because everybody out there is a great player (or they wouldn't be there), everyone can learn something by observing everyone else. Believe me, there is a lot of looking going on. In fact, the great Sam Snead, tired of hearing so much spoken and written about Ben Hogan's alleged "secret," once quipped, "There are no secrets in golf, everybody's looking!"

Speaking of Sam, I had the pleasure of playing with him in the 1979 Masters, having qualified for the event by virtue of being a semifinalist in the 1978 U.S. Amateur championship. Today, only the winner and runner-up of the amateur tournament earn a trip to Augusta; but, back then, all four semifinalists got to go. I was just shy of my nineteenth birthday, and Sam was sixty-five, so I was a bit surprised when he told me not to call him Mr. Snead. "I look around for my daddy when you say 'Mr. Snead'," Sam said. *Daddy?* I remember thinking. *He could be my grandfather!*

But he sure didn't have a grandfatherly golf swing, I can assure you of that. Still present and accounted for was his unbelievable sense of rhythm and his impeccable timing, and though the years had subtracted a few yards from his driver, they did nothing to muffle the riflelike sound with which his shots came off of the club face. I found the masterly way he controlled the trajectory of his shots and the straightness of his drives mind-boggling. Of course, Sam's swing still displayed the incredible style and grace that many still consider the best golf swing ever. I consider it one of golf's most intriguing ironies, that here we have golf's greatest stylist—and he was someone who never had a formal instructor indoctrinating him with the superficialities of swing style. Sam learned his swing the old-fashioned way: He figured it out dynamic by dynamic, all on his own.

So, I was paired with Sam in the second round of the Masters, having shot 73 in the opening round. We played three holes, before a line of thunderstorms came through on a cold front, and play was suspended. I can't begin to tell you how much I enjoyed our relaxed, three-hour lunch in Augusta National's storied clubhouse. People know Sam, of course, as one of the game's greatest players and swingers, but they don't realize that he was also a world-class raconteur who could spin a golf yarn with the best of them. But, speaking with Sam, whom I had always idolized, during that rain delay helped me get to know him as a human being who was not that different from me, and that made me much more comfortable when we went back out to play.

In fact, when we did resume, I started playing really well. I'll never forget when we teed off on the par-5 thirteenth hole, with Rae's Creek tracking the length of the hole down the left side. I had been working the ball in both directions real well that year, and I hit a nice, high draw shot around the corner. Sam wasn't hitting it that long, being sixty-five, and his drive came to rest about forty yards behind mine. So he laid up with a 5-iron and walked up toward me, where I was waiting for the green to clear, and said, "You damn college kids; I'm hitting a five-iron to lay up, and you're hitting a five-iron to go for the green." He was kind of playing with me, you see. I hit my five-iron on the edge of the green, and as soon as my ball landed up there, he was over his wedge, which he hit to a foot from the hole. Sam walked around that tributary into which Rae's Creek flows and tapped in for his birdie before I even got to the green!

Next, we got to the fifteenth hole. It was pushing eight o'clock, and it was getting dark, so I said, "Sam, don't you think it's a little too dark for us to continue playing?" He just said, "You keep on playing."

We played hole fifteen and got to the sixteenth tee, and by then it was so dark you could just see the silhouette of the pond on the left of this beautiful par-3 hole, and the outline of the bunkers behind the green. You could just barely see the flagstick.

So I said to him, "Sam, don't you really think it's too dark to play?" to which he said again, "Keep on playing, son."

What was I supposed to do? Say, "Sam, I know more about this than you do." I don't think so.

So, we got to the seventeenth hole, and all you could see was the silhouette of what the club's members call Ike's tree out there (because President Eisenhower, a true golf lover, often hit that tree with his drive when he played the course), and I hit my tee shot. We were walking down the fairway when I said, "Sam, really, this is nighttime!"

You guessed it. He answered, "Keep on playing until they come out here with the members and tell us to go in."

Before I could hit my second shot, I had to walk all the way up to the green to see where the pin was, in relation to the bunker, because the only thing I could see from the fairway was the bunker. I got the yardage, and I ended up hitting an 8-iron four feet from the hole, kind of like the shot Tiger hit years later in the dark at Firestone, right next to the pin. Of course, Tiger's shot sealed the tournament victory for him, while I was doing my best to make the cut.

I then had a four-footer for birdie, and it was so dark that I had no idea about any aspect of the break. I even laid my hands spread-eagle on the green, trying to feel which side of the ground was higher than the other, but that didn't help. So I asked my caddie, who worked year-round at Augusta National, "How does this green normally break?" I figured he'd know. He said, "I like it about a ball outside the right edge," meaning the ball would then break back and into the hole. That's where I stroked it, a ball outside of the hole, on the right. Well, it broke about another cup to the right, the opposite way in which the caddie said it would. He obviously couldn't see anything either. When they finally came up to say it was too dark to play, I managed to putt in for my par, which was my prerogative to do, and then we headed in.

Sam, of course, wasn't going to make the cut, and I've wondered whether the powers that be at Augusta extended our long day's journey into night, hoping we could finish our round, so Sam could pack up and get out of town without having to return the next morning to finish what, for him, would have been a meaningless few holes. I'll never know, and it doesn't really matter.

When I got to the clubhouse (it's a miracle we found *that*!) I found out that my score of even-par for the day, one over for the thirty-five holes I'd played in the tournament, put me exactly on the cut line. They scheduled Sam and me to come back at eight the next morning to play hole eighteen, and to complete our second round, which meant I had to sleep on parring the eighteenth at Augusta National, to make the cut in my first Masters. That one hole might not have meant anything to the great Sam Snead, but it meant everything to me.

I couldn't sleep hardly a wink, as, all night long, I was mulling over how I would play that eighteenth hole. I decided I would take the fairway bunkers out of play by hitting a 3-wood off the tee, which would leave me a 6-iron to the green. So, that's all I hit on the practice tee early on Saturday morning, 3-woods and 6-irons.

Maybe it was sleep deprivation, or some kind of divine intervention, but as I was walking back down the eighteenth fairway towards the tee to play the hole, the thought came to me that, every time I hit a 3-wood during a practice round, on the eighteenth I made bogie. Doubt had crept in, and I suddenly found myself dealing with that doubt, without a lot of real estate over which to do it, until I reached the tee box to hit my drive.

I decided to deal with this doubt by making a very positive swing with my driver. In other words, I was going to play aggressive, not protective or defensive golf, which hitting the safe 3-wood shot would have represented. What I was still too sleepy to realize, thank God, was that I hadn't hit even one driver that morning on the range. I took a couple of practice swings, then hit this perfect little power cut, right up in the middle between the bunkers, then hit an 8-iron to about fifteen feet just right of the hole where I was trying to hit it, and made the putt for a birdie three. I had made the cut with a stroke to spare. All the patrons gathered around the green gave me a standing ovation, which was really cool.

Sam didn't go to the practice tee that morning, but I still remember walking down the hill of eighteen, back to the tee, and seeing Sam hitting balls off the back of it, toward Rae's Creek, to warm up, which they allowed you to do back then. In fact, these two great icons of our game, Augusta National and Sam Snead, with that gorgeous swing of his, hitting those warm-up balls, have engraved themselves in my mind, for me to recall whenever I wish, which I do with great pleasure each April, when I return to call the event with the rest of the CBS golf crew.

The only reason I beat Sam that week was because I hit the ball so much farther than he did, and the only reason I did that was because I was eighteen and he was sixty-five years old. He was still a great shot-maker, and with the sidesaddle method of putting, he putted beautifully, as well. As I said, any time you play with someone better than you, you can learn from him or her.

What I learned from Sam was that the golf swing is a fluid, continuous, blended motion, and not a bunch of connected dots. His impact position was incredibly dynamic, and something to behold, and with that flat left wrist, he compressed the ball beautifully, with divots that extended exactly four inches in front. Heck, even well into his eighties, when he no longer competed in the Masters, and he, Byron Nelson, and Gene Sarazen would hit the ceremonial first drives off number one to open the tournament, he still swung beautifully and hit the ball great. In fact, it's absolutely clear to me now that an uninhibited, free-flowing swing like Sam's functions as a kind of fountain of youth, which keeps the body limber and the mind sharp. That's what a lifetime of developing great dynamics can do for you and your golf swing!

Now, let's look at each one of our five dynamics specifically, and the swings with which we've partnered them in this book, and examine the thinking, feeling, imagining, and psychological issues that accompany them. This is to say, let's continue to explore golf's mental dynamics.

DYNAMIC #1: PUTTING AND THE FLAT LEFT WRIST AT IMPACT

You began your journey toward a dynamics-based swing with putting and the number-one dynamic, a flat left wrist at impact. Putting presents this dynamic in a relatively simple way, because, when putting, you want your left wrist to be flat, both in the address and the impact positions, and because the putting stroke is so small. Therefore, the first mental exercise that putting assigns you is simply to *look, look, look! Look* at how the flat left wrist forms a straight line from the left shoulder, down the arm, and to the putter shaft itself.

Homer Kelley, in *The Golfing Machine,* instructed his readers to fix in their minds the body's and the club's alignments at impact, beginning with a flat left wrist. Let's use a more contemporary, information-age image, and *burn* that image of a flat left wrist at impact onto an impact zone's CD in your minds.

As I've said throughout these pages, the number-one culprit that blurs, if not obliterates, this mental image of a flat left wrist at impact is the ball. Even before that very curious species of thinkers, called sports, or golf, psychologists, blossomed on the game scene, every serious player knew and feared that dreaded mental disease of putting, called "the yips." What are the yips? An acronym for the yips might be "Yanked Impulsive Pressure Surges." More plainly, it's an uncontrollable, convulsive, neurologically based urge *to hit at the ball,* expressed in a spastic, twitching muscle action that destroys the flat left wrist at impact, and delivers the putter to the ball with too much speed, and at an erratic pace. I'm sad to say that I've played with pros who were facing a simple, straight-in, three-foot putt, and yipped the ball practically off the green!

Indeed, nothing destroys a smooth putting stroke (and a flat left wrist at impact) more than excessive or obsessive attention to the ball. Take the ball away from a yipping putter and that person will make a beautiful, smooth stroke almost every time. Therefore, you need to redirect your attention away from the ball and back to your hands as they direct your stroke through the ball with that flat left wrist. To me, this is the most important value of the practice stroke that I, and most pros, use prior to hitting a putt. Practice strokes direct your attention away from the ball and into your flat left wrist. We need to view clearly the image of that flat left wrist that we have burned into your mind before your stroke began. In other words, your mind needs to be directed more to visualizing the motion than to applying that motion during the stroke itself. As your preshot and in-shot visualization of your dynamic improves, so will your putting stroke. When striking the putt, make a conscious effort to duplicate the practice stroke taken earlier.

I was working on my putting the other day, and I began to feel a bit of a hit at the ball, rather than a smooth stroke through it. It wasn't a full-blown yip, by any means, but it came from the same ball-focused region of the brain as the yips do, so it signaled an alarm in me to make some practice strokes without the ball. As I focused on keeping the pressure in my hands constant throughout the impact interval, I improved almost immediately.

Any pressure change in the grip while putting, then, is an attempt to *hit* at the ball. Call it what you will, i.e., steering, hitting, or throwing the club head lag away, this breaks down our number-one dynamic of a flat left wrist at impact.

Of course, while there can't be any pressure change at all in the hands with any shot in golf, you can notice its destructive effects when putting—again, because the putt is such a small stroke, and the club moves so slowly.

During my early days on tour, I often roomed and played practice rounds with Johnny Miller. Johnny and I are both from northern California, and we both went to BYU, so he was sort of a big brother to me back then. I remember him telling me that when he shot his famous 63 at Oakmont, on his way to the 1973 U.S. Open title, he had one thought while putting: to keep his right wrist bent at the same angle all through the stroke and especially through impact. (It helped, too, that he remembered to bring his yardage book to the golf course that day. The day before, he had forgotten it and shot 76.)

In our putting chapter, we talked about the relation between the flat left wrist and the bent right wrist. To review, a flat left wrist insures a bent right wrist and a bent right wrist insures a flat left wrist. Though these phrases create a bit of a tongue twister, an incorrect bent left wrist at impact automatically flattens the right wrist, which is what Johnny Miller fixed by remaining mindful of keeping that wrist bent through the entire stroke (i.e., the impact zone).

The bigger picture finds that Johnny used his visual imagination in a manner that, for him, worked best to insure a flat left wrist dynamic at impact. It's worth pointing out that Johnny (like Ben Hogan, Curtis Strange, and a number of other great golfers) is left-handed. Therefore, his right hand represents his weaker, or less athletic, hand, which understandably requires more of his attention during his stroke. The moral here is that it doesn't matter what you imagine or think of to produce good dynamics through the impact zone, it only matters that you perceive the necessity of applying your mind to direct your body to execute and produce them soundly.

After winning that U.S. Open title, Johnny Miller went into a putting slump. His stroke became jabby, and his left wrist began to break down slightly. For all intents and purposes, he developed a case of the yips. Had he continued to stroke his putts with his mind on his hands, focused on not changing the pressure in his grip, he would have been able to maintain his dynamics. Finally, in 1976 his putting was so bad that he tried looking at the hole while stroking the putt. He would set up normally then shift his eyes away from the ball and to the hole before making his stroke. Few realize that he won the British Open that year never looking at the ball while putting.

Johnny found a creative cure for a flawed Number-One Dynamic. Since he was so ball-bound or ball-conscious in his putting, his stroke found restitution when he totally eliminated the ball from his view. Though this procedure was quite unorthodox, Johnny made it work and, in so doing, proved the value of maintaining the Number-One Dynamic at all costs. Many pros have followed suit and stroked putts while looking at the hole. Davis Love nearly does this, but he brings his eyes back to the ball just a split second before he begins his putting stroke. The net effect is the same. The longer one looks at the ball, the more the potential of becoming ball-bound. Loren Roberts, "The Boss of the Moss," frees himself of ball-boundedness by standing over the ball and intensely gazing at a dimple on the front of it, until the ball almost blurs away from view, before beginning his stroke. Whatever you need to do to be less focused on the ball, do it!

DYNAMIC #2: CHIPPING AND THE FORWARD SWING BOTTOM (AND THE FORWARD-LEANING CLUB SHAFT AT IMPACT)

I'm sure some of you are old enough to remember the fun of watching a Polaroid snapshot slowly developing, detail by detail, right in front of your eyes. Similarly, the mental image of your swing's dynamics grows and clarifies, piece by piece. This means that, with chipping, you want to add to your picture of Dynamic Number One, the flat left wrist at impact, the image of a forward swing bottom, with a forward-leaning club shaft at impact. With chipping, you want to strike down on the ball to hit it up, however minimally, into the air; and to assure that you do so dynamically, you need to make sure that the bottom of your swing arc falls in front of the ball a good four inches. This also insures that your club shaft will lean forward at impact as well. Actually, it's a bit of a chicken-or-egg thing, because, if your club shaft leans forward correctly, you will automatically hit down on the ball, with a divot in front of the ball.

What's more, if your left wrist breaks down at impact, you will have created a club head that swings up and in (instead of down and forward), and the divot will start at or behind the ball, with the handle of the club and the shaft tilting back, not forward, at impact. So, you can again see how the dynamics intersect and interrelate with one another, and how, as we learn to execute and integrate them, they form one unified picture of the golf swing.

Let's work backward a bit, and purposely make an undynamic chipping stroke, meaning, one that allows the left wrist to break down through the impact zone. Pick up a wedge and make such a swing yourself. Observe how the shaft tilts back. Now, pose or fix yourself in the correct impact-alignment position for chipping,

Note the forward lean of the club shaft, the divot's starting point at the line, and the forward swing bottom. The perfect divot starts at the line (which represents the ball), and the bottom, or deepest point, of it extends four inches in front of the line. *(Photo by Kerry Corcoran.)*

which means a flat left wrist and the shaft leaning forward. Observe how the forward lean of the club shaft can do nothing but direct your club head down, through, and forward on the ball, as your stroke flows through the impact zone. It makes all the sense in the world, doesn't it, to get your golf club moving forward, not backward, through the impact zone?

Once more, Jack Nicklaus talks about intentionally making

incorrect motions or swings during some of his practice sessions (as I just asked you to do in the above exercise), in order to feel the difference between the correct and incorrect swing dynamics on which he is working. We all know that no one has had better mental dynamics in the history of golf than Jack Nicklaus!

Indeed, all of your dynamics strive to move the bottom of your swing arc well in front of the ball. While I've discussed at length many of the reasons why golfers struggle to do this, I've saved the more mental and/or perceptual reasons for this chapter. First of all, standing on the side of the ball, as you do in golf, creates an optical illusion that the club shaft leans *more forward* at impact, as the golfer perceives it, than it really does.

In other words, the illusion makes you think that the club is way too far forward at impact when it is barely leaning forward at all! Therefore, I contend that, as long as you keep the head steady through the impact zone on all shots, including the chip, you can't at all have the feeling or the visual sensation that the shaft is leaning too far forward. In short, it never will.

What's more, this feeling that the shaft is leaning too far forward at impact, when chipping, can actually alarm a lot of golfers, to the degree that they will break down their left wrist and throw the club head away, in an attempt to back the shaft up to a more comfortable-looking, straight-up-and-down relationship to the ground. Again, the center of gravity on all golf clubs (also called the "sweet spot") seeks to align itself with the shaft at impact on all swings. When the flat left wrist breaks down, and the sweet spot passes the shaft, physics dictates that acceleration will dramatically slow down, to return the shaft and sweet spot to a straight alignment.

The point to digest here is that, when chipping, as when putting, you want your address and impact positions to be virtually identical, and that means with a flat left wrist for both shots. You address the chip shot, and not the putt, with the shaft leaning more forward, to insure that you strike down on the ball with a forward swing bottom, in order to produce height on the shot. Of course, some players do make the stylistic choice to address their putts with the shaft leaning forward as well. Remember, as I said, one of the game's best putters, Dave Stockton, addresses and strikes his putts with the shaft leaning noticeably forward, and uses a high-lofted putter to compensate for the delofting effect his technique produces. Phil Mickelson does the same, and is known to use a putter with 5 degrees of loft, which is a bit higher than the average loft on putters on tour.

Because a chipping stroke strongly resembles a putting stroke, people can also have the yips while chipping. Appropriately, we call one version of a yipped chip a "chili dip," because it describes a convulsive (spicy?), jerky motion and impact that drops, or "dips," the club sharply behind the ball. Often, it's poor mental dynamics that causes this error, because golfers erroneously think that they have to get the club head under the ball and then lift it into the air, as if they were scooping the ball up with a small shovel (perhaps we should rename this error the "double-dip," as in an ice cream cone). You must always remember that a downward blow (i.e., with a swing bottom well in front of the ball) gets the ball up in the air because the ball contacts the club higher up on its face. This launches the shot at a higher angle, with increased backspin, which adds even more lift to the flight of the ball.

Actually, the average golfer's instinct to get the club head under the ball is sound and reasonable, because one has to swing down to get the club head low enough into the ground, so that the ball strikes the club high enough on its face to fly up. But the club must swing *forward as well as down*. That's why we name our Second Dynamic the *forward swing bottom*, and not just the swing bottom.

We saw that performing the sand drill, even with a short

chipping stroke, produces a divot whose center is four inches in front of the ball. Remember though, that, while the sand gives way easily during the sand drill, you don't want to take a deep or a gouging divot while chipping. In other words, even a shallow divot's center can lie four inches in front of the ball.

I also introduced the aiming point technique in the chipping chapter. To review, the aiming point technique has you aim your club and hands, at the completion of your backstroke, to a point forward of the ball, located on your straight plane line. This procedure takes a little bit of mental practice and training, because, again, it's counterintuitive to aim the club at something other than the ball. But, in order to achieve a swing bottom well in front of the ball on all shots (other than putts), it makes sense to aim the club forward of the ball as well, and the aiming point technique is designed specifically to let the club head swing down and through, to that forward swing bottom location.

DYNAMIC #3: THE PITCH SHOT
AND LOADING

When pitching, you want the club, at address, to point to your belt buckle, in what might be called a "middle-of-the-body" position, which bends (or cups) the flat left wrist you used when addressing putts and chips. In other words, when pitching, address and impact are two distinctively different positions.

As I said, the pitch shot is truly a small full swing, and therefore, you want to set or load the club almost fully during the pitch swing. This centered-shaft, bent-left-wrist position at address makes it easier to do so, and loading the club well does much to insure a flat left wrist at impact, and a forward swing bottom four inches in front of the ball.

Here's an exercise that will help you really feel this: Set up to a shot in the pitching address position, then, without making a swing, shift forward into impact, then, alternately, back to address. Doing this several times in succession will help you burn into your mind both the image at impact when pitching and the fact that, because of its longer swing, we arrive at impact more dynamically when pitching.

Because the pitch and full swings have so much in common (try running a video tape of a tour pro pitching in slow motion, and you'll be hard-pressed to distinguish this swing from a full swing), much of what I say in this part of the chapter applies to full swings with any club, as well.

For example, an interesting psychological issue that emerges for the first time with pitching, and most certainly carries into swinging, is the perhaps instinctual fear many golfers have of swinging the club down into the ground. Some golfers I've spoken with explicitly express a queasy sense of violating Mother Earth when taking a divot. But this fear has to be resolved because, on a truly well-struck golf shot, starting with the chip, the golfer must

 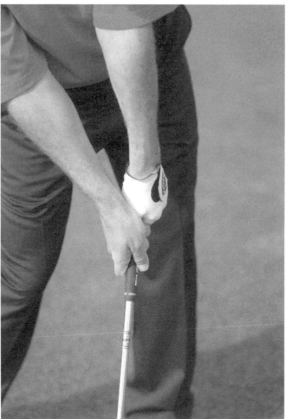

When struggling with getting a clear vision of the proper impact dynamics, I return to this drill of shifting my hands and the club shaft from the address to the impact positions, because it burns the correct image of a hands-ahead, flat left wrist and a forward lean of the club shaft impact position clearly in my mind. I know the clearer the picture is in my head, the more effectively I can accomplish dynamic impact in my swing. *(Photos by Kerry Corcoran.)*

swing the club into the ground (unless, of course the ball starts well-elevated on a tee, as it usually does when hitting a driver).

Again, though we do strike down on the ball when chipping, it is with pitching that for the first time we really hit somewhat aggressively into the ground and take a healthy divot.

Another reason why people hesitate to hit down into the ground is that they have learned the game with poor dynamics. Therefore, from the start they have swing bottoms that fall behind the ball, instead of in front of it. Sure, they have been told before to take a divot, and, indeed, they have tried to strike down into the ground. In fact, many do a good enough job of it, only, again, they hit the ground with their club well behind the ball. So, naturally, they develop a fear of taking a divot, because they know from experience that when they do so, they hit a lousy, fat shot.

However, instead of correcting the problem of their faulty swing bottom by employing good dynamics to move it forward, these golfers try to fix it by avoiding the ground altogether, by breaking down their left wrists at impact, in an attempt to cleanly scoop the ball into the air. The more their dynamics break down, the farther behind the ball falls the bottom of their swing arc, and the farther behind the ball they hit the ground, the more they unconsciously break down their dynamics, in an attempt to swing up and not down on the ball. Certainly, golfers may succeed in raising the whole level of their swing arc higher off the ground in their efforts not to hit the ball fat, but when that happens, they simply skull the ball thinly at its midsection. So, fat and thin shots represent two sides of a vicious cycle that keeps

these golfers from ever developing good swing dynamics or ever improving.

Now let's review what happens when you do indeed correctly strike down on the ball with a forward swing bottom. When you hit down and forward, you contact the ball higher on the club face, and the higher you hit the ball on the face, the higher the ball will go.

However, on the practice range I would rather see a golfer hit a fat shot than a thin one. At least a fat shot has the force of the swing going into the ground, though impact is still too far behind the point where it needs to be. What's more, as the club properly enters into the ground at impact, the turf itself slows down the club head through resistance, and the feeling of structural support this produces in the golfer's hands actually encourages the desired flat left wrist, forward hands, and forward-leaning club shaft through the impact zone. As these golfers work on getting their swing bottom more forward, they will see immediate positive results. If they try to fix their problem by missing the ground, they will never see the results they are hoping to achieve. Again, you have to have a clear mental image of dynamic-impact geometry, and learn from experience to trust that hitting down, not up, on the ball drives it solidly into the air.

In fact, I, too, have struggled with this fear of hitting fat shots, and I've noticed that the more I play and hit balls, the more real this fear becomes. Recently, I was preparing for a tournament in the winter. The air was cold, the ground was wet, and as I was practicing some 4-iron shots, I realized I was hitting the vast number of them thin. Let me tell you, those thin shots didn't feel too good in that cold weather! I stopped for a minute to ponder why I was hitting so many thin shots, then realized that several things were happening: One, I had become too ball-conscious, instead of focusing my attention to my aiming point in front of the ball. Two, the wet, soupy soil increased my fear of hitting into the ground, as I can't stand having to pluck mud out of my eye or to change out of a mud-stained sweater. Three, I subconsciously thought that if I shallowed-out my hit with a long iron, and kind of picked or swept the ball clean off the ground and up into the air, I'd hit my shots higher. But this was faulty thinking, which I needed to change.

So I grabbed that 4-iron again, headed into the practice sand bunker, and began to make some very aggressive full-practice swings, challenging myself to take as big a divot in front of the imaginary ball as possible. I focused on setting, or loading, the club on the backswing and sustaining or even increasing the lag

on the downswing. After ten minutes of this I was ready to hit balls again, making sure I kept that same aggressive thought of hitting into the ground and directing my aiming point four inches in front of the ball to insure a forward swing bottom. My ball striking improved immediately *simply because I improved my dynamics!*

The goal of hitting down and through the ball, creating a healthy divot that extends four to five inches in front of the ball, raises the important issue of practicing off driving range mats, where one literally cannot take (or, obviously, observe) a divot at all. For this reason, practicing shots off of these mats can be detrimental to developing good dynamics, but it doesn't have to be. It all goes back again to being *mindful*. In other words, you can still have an effective practice session hitting off of mats if you use your sense of feel in your hands to tell you where the bottom of your swing arc falls.

Certainly, it's much more difficult to feel your swing's bottom off a mat, because it doesn't give you the feedback of a divot that grass provides. So, it's important to find newer and better quality

Pages 204-207: Tiger Woods plays an iron shot. You can see that he almost violently attacks the ground with a decisively aggressive downward blow. I guess that's one reason they call him Tiger. *(Photos by Warren Keating. Used with the permission of the PGA Tour and CBS Sports.)*

mats from which to practice, because these do, in fact, give a little at impact and allow the club to begin to swing down and forward, as it should.

However, mats, because of the jarring impact they produce, can make golfers naturally shy away from striking down on the ball in the first place. Therefore, it's really best to search out a driving range in your area that has good grass-hitting bays, even if it takes you a little longer to get there. Most driving ranges don't charge more for hitting off grass, though some do.

Let's look at some social concerns and scenarios that discourage golfers from taking divots. You swing down when practicing inside, and your spouse will get mad at you for scraping the floor, threatening the carpet, or just making noise. You do it in the yard, and you've got to pay the gardener to repair the lawn.

A friend and I went out to the range the other day and I began by taking practice swings, complete, of course, with divots.

"What are you doing?" my friend asked.

"I want to take a divot on my real swing, don't I? So why wouldn't I take one with my practice swing?"

Being told (or imagining such reprimands) not to take divots when playing or practicing golf is like being told not to hit the pins when you go bowling!

Since we agree that divots are indeed very good things, let's look at the different types of divots created by short and long irons. Because short irons have angled-back club faces, their centers of gravity push the club heads sharply down toward the ground through the impact zone, which results in a relatively deep divot. In addition, the short iron's shorter shaft creates a steep angle of attack into the ball, which leads to deeper divots as well. Long irons and fairway woods, on the other hand, have centers of gravity that work more horizontally, or forward, through the ball, and their longer shafts create flatter approach angles through the impact zone, and shallower divots. Therefore, while all divots should extend four inches in front of the ball, those taken with short irons will naturally be a bit deeper than those taken with long irons.

As for driver shots hit off of a tee, I like the expression "air divot" for the imaginary space displaced by the downward motion of the club head, immediately after it passes the ball en route to its forward swing bottom.

Before closing this pitch shot section of the "Mental Dynamics" chapter, you need to recognize the negative effect tension has on loading the club fully and well, on both pitch and full shots. Tension, a side effect of nervousness, obviously tightens your muscles and really inhibits, if not destroys, the full cocking of the left wrist during the backswing. Just as tension tightens our muscles, remembering to grip the club with secure fingers and relaxed wrists reduces the amount of tension in the hands, arms, and throughout the body.

Andy Brumer once asked Tom Watson in an interview how he broke through on the PGA Tour and learned to win consistently. Tom answered, "When I learned how to breathe correctly on the golf course." Indeed, Yoga masters have known for centuries of the link between proper breathing and muscle relaxation, and should any of them play (or take up) golf, I suspect they would load the club very well.

DYNAMIC #4: LAG AND THE FULL SWING

As I've said, the pitch and the full swing have much in common mechanically, and, therefore, they share many of the same mental dynamics as well. First of all, we want to remind ourselves that, when swinging, as when pitching, address and impact represent different positions. For the sake of review, let's repeat the same drill we did above, just so we really understand and feel this difference.

Start by placing yourself in the full swing's impact position, with your left wrist flat, the club shaft leaning forward, your hips slightly open, and your head just behind the ball. Set or, as we said, "burn" that visual image of impact into your memory, so you can swing through it when actually hitting shots. Next, return to address by squaring your hips, realigning the shaft to a center-of-the-body, or belt-buckle position, and allowing your left wrist to bend or cup. Now, shift back and forth between address and impact, so you can learn, see, and feel the difference between the two positions.

Interestingly, lag in your full swing even has something in common with putting, because throwing or casting your lag away at the top of the full swing resembles the putting yips. Both errors lead to the breaking down of the flat left wrist at impact, and both spring from the instinct to hit at the ball, instead of making a smooth swinging motion through the impact zone.

This is why the transition period between the end of the backswing and the start of the downswing represents such an important segment of the full swing. During this interval, your change of direction deposits the club against the pressure point of your right forefinger to establish your swing's lag. From a mental dynamics perspective, now is when you must become mindful of storing and preserving that lag through the impact zone.

In other words, the full swing's lagging action really allows golfers to feel that club head in their hands. In fact, when golfers load and lag the club head well, they feel that their hands and the club head have become one. Therefore, at the top of the swing, the mind shifts its attention to the hands, and to retaining the club head's lag intact, right through the impact zone.

Ben Hogan said that impact should be incidental to the swing, which means that, from the moment we begin to lag our loaded power on the downswing, we should make no yip, hitch, jerk, or any accommodation whatsoever for the ball. In other words, we swing smoothly through impact and not at the ball.

Remember, swing style is an expression of swing dynamics, and not the other way around. For example, all dynamic swingers lag a fully loaded club through the impact zone, but different players set or establish this load in a range of styles. Johnny Miller, Nick Faldo, Corey Pavin, and the promising young PGA Tour player Ryan Moore set the club very early in their backswings, to establish their load. Tiger Woods, Vijay Singh, David Toms, Luke Donald, and countless others set or load the club gradually, so that, by the middle of their backswings, they have completed the job. Jack Nicklaus, the late Payne Stewart, Bob Tway, and Sergio Garcia set and load the club very late in their backswings.

Sergio Garcia's swing, for example, displays a rather violent transition, from the top of the backswing to the beginning of the downswing, during which Sergio simultaneously finishes the backswing loading of his club and begins to strongly lag it toward the impact zone. Many of the great teachers in the game stood perplexed when they first saw Sergio, in his early years on tour, create so much lag during the initial stage of his downswing that his shaft laid off the plane 20 degrees or so. They were even more confused when he became the leading total driver (combined distance and accuracy) on the PGA Tour, especially with the club in such a laid-off start at the downswing position. Sergio has since modified his swing, and now loads the club a little earlier in his backswing, which helps him get the club more on-plane throughout his full swing.

Some people have made a big deal about Sergio's swing

Pages 211–212: Sergio's strong loading and lagging of the club promotes great swing dynamics, and, as you can see here, an on-plane delivery of the club through the impact zone, where it counts. These pictures are proof positive once again that good dynamics should be taught and mastered long before the swing plane or anything else, though this point of view lies in direct contrast to how many golf instructors teach the game today. *(Photos by Warren Keating. Used with the permission of the PGA Tour and CBS Sports.)*

change, but the truth is, it didn't change his dynamics at all. While he doesn't load the club with as vigorous a look as he reaches the top of his backswing, as he did in years past, he may actually now *increase* his lag even more during the downswing than he did before. In short, he still lags the club with the best of them on his downswing. In fact, if there were a statistical category for lagging the golf club, Sergio would most likely be its leader.

DYNAMIC #5: THE STRAIGHT PLANE LINE AND THE ISSUE OF TARGET-CONSCIOUSNESS

A golfer's ultimate goal is to stand over the shot, see the target, and think about nothing else. Excellent swing dynamics frees you to become more target-conscious in this way. "When I'm playing well, I don't even aim," said Fred Couples. That's taking the ultimate goal to the ultimate level. However, as much as we enjoy the fantasy of Fred Couples, as a completely natural golfer who was born with a silver swing in his genes, even he didn't develop his great swing dynamics overnight.

In fact, focusing your mind on your target before you have developed the level of swing dynamics necessary to do so actually decreases your accuracy, because it causes you to stiffly steer or guide the club, rather than lag it, in a free-flowing, freewheeling motion through the impact zone. Steering means consciously trying to place the club directly on top of the straight plane line through the impact zone, rather than lagging it from inside that line, and it results in a casting or throw-away motion that destroys both your flat left wrist at impact and your forward swing bottom.

I remember Ben Doyle and I once having a discussion about alignment. I was in my typical, perfectionist personality mode, splitting hairs on my alignment and getting all caught up with where my feet were aimed and where my hips and shoulders were pointing at address. Ben responded by pulling out a 5-iron from his assorted bag of tricks and, dropping three balls on the ground, he hit each ball with no regard to how far left he was aiming. Then he said, "That's where I was aimed!" He then turned about 30 degrees to the right and hit another ball. "That's where I was aimed!" he said again. Once more, he turned 30 degrees to the right, hit, and said, "That's where I was aimed!"

Ben's demonstrations left me wondering, what was his point?

He often teaches using parable-style language like this, full of extra, though seemingly hidden wisdom, and I had to ponder it a
moment before I got it. Contrary to how most golfers are taught,
feet, hips, and shoulders do not determine where you are aimed.
Rather, you determine your true ball-to-target aiming line (or the
line on which you want to start your shot) by mentally con-

You establish proper alignment at address by constructing the mental image of a line
toward you from the ball to a spot in which you have positioned the ball between
your feet, and by extending another line perpendicular to this one starting from the
ball and aimed straight at your target. *(Photo by Kerry Corcoran.)*

structing, or "drawing," a perpendicular (90-degree) angle from your ball-placement location between your feet (I position most of my full shots three inches inside my left heel) to the ball, then another line at a right angle to that line. Where this second line is pointing is where you are aimed. Whether your feet, hips, or shoulders are closed or open is not that critical: What matters is that you direct this mental image of a T-square, or right angle, so the ball-to-target part of it points directly at your target.

We call the straight plane line dynamic our "guiding dynamic" because it provides us with the visual image of a straight line running through the ball to our target (or, again, to the line on which we want to start our shot). It is in relation to this line that we want to swing our club through the impact zone. Fred Couples's comment that, when he's playing well, he doesn't really aim, isn't as cryptic as it may sound. What he means is, after aligning

Though Fred Couples has a less-than-conventional setup/address position, with open feet, open hips, and open shoulders, he nevertheless derives his aim by drawing a perpendicular line from his ball placement, to the ball, to the target. Even with his so-called open setup, Freddy still swings the club on-plane straight to his target (i.e., to the right of, not parallel to, his body alignment) through the impact zone. *(Photos by Warren Keating. Used with the permission of the PGA Tour and CBS Sports.)*

himself to his target via his straight plane line, he *is free* to forget about his target (be it the flagstick or a section of the fairway) on a conscious level, and focuses instead on making a good, dynamic swing, in relation to his straight plane line. Therefore, his hands know where to swing the club, regardless of where he has aligned his body.

As I said in the straight plane line dynamics chapter, indoor practice into a net is a good way to direct your attention to your dynamics, without becoming distracted, or mesmerized, by the ball's flight and/or the shot's target. As a young teenager learning golf in Freeport, New York, my writing partner Andy Brumer practiced hitting balls into a net on his screened porch. That is, until his dad came down in his sleeping gown at three A.M. and took the club out of Andy's hands. It seemed the *thwack, thwack* of Andy's well-struck shots was keeping his parents awake. The next morning, when Andy came downstairs for breakfast, he found that net packed away in the box in which it came. But Andy now has excellent swing dynamics, and he enthusiastically agrees that they're getting better as a result of his coauthoring this book!

The straight plane line has a unique, and, indeed, remarkable capacity to unify all of our dynamics, because swinging on-plane allows us to lag the club through the impact zone, and to strike the ball with a flat left wrist and a forward swing bottom. As you begin to understand and experience the Fifth Dynamic's unifying role, the entire picture of a fully dynamic swing will brighten and clarify in your mind's eye.

DYNAMIC PRACTICE: FROM PERFECTION TO PROGRESSIVE IMPROVEMENT

The very idea of practice serves as a metaphor for a mentally dynamic game, because it is during practice that you use your creative mind to understand and apply new technical aspects of the swing. As Ben Doyle says, understanding and execution represent two halves of the same puzzle that long to come together. The practice tee, the living room mirror (as well as other less obvious venues—or props, such as an umbrella to swing) serve as the testing grounds where you work to integrate and join your understanding and execution into one dynamic motion. Jack Nicklaus has written that, when he is out practicing and not hitting the ball as well as he would like, he doesn't mindlessly beat a lot of golf balls to solve his problem. Instead, he packs up his clubs and heads home, where, in the comfort of his favorite upholstered chair, he visualizes his swing and reasons through to an effective solution.

As I've said, the sandy soil amongst the trees at Pinehurst served as my practice laboratory, where my full understanding of the swing's dynamics came together in my mind. While some say that "practice makes perfect," and others that "practice makes permanent," I believe that practice moves us away from unrealistic fantasies of perfection, and toward the far more realistic (and therefore gratifying) goal of progressive improvement. Again, from a mental dynamics vantage point, what we want to improve is our capacity to see ourselves making dynamic swings through the impact zone. Here's another saying that I like: *Today's preparation is tomorrow's performance,* because its forward-looking philosophy corresponds to our ultimate goal of achieving a forward swing bottom through the impact zone.

Practice drills have become very popular among all levels of golfers because they integrate sound swing mechanics and the means to produce them. Speaking of drills, many people have the wrong idea about Vijay Singh's practice sessions. They think that all he does is go to the range every day and beat balls for hours on end. Well, you don't become the number-one player in the world, as Vijay did not too long ago, by mindlessly hitting golf balls until your fingers bleed. In fact, Vijay spends as much time doing drills on the range as he does actually hitting balls.

For every group of five or six balls he may hit in a row, he'll take a break and spend as much time doing drills. I recommend this fifty-fifty ratio for all golfers. Vijay's drills serve as a means to his singular end of improving his swing dynamics, and his comprehensive training program also includes studying his swing on video, as well as a rigorous fitness regimen. As good as Vijay is, he believes that he can get better, which is a mindset he shares with Tiger Woods. If two of the best players in the world think of improvement as a never-ending, lifelong journey, and not an end in itself, shouldn't the rest of us give up the nagging ghost of perfection and enjoy such a ride with them, as well?

Vijay's practice station on the range looks like a cross between the training aid section of your local golf merchandise retail outlet and an inventor's studio. He's got headless shafts that he uses for alignment and swing-plane drills, a heavily weighted club with which he does strengthening and swing-rhythm drills, old golf gloves that he puts under his armpits for pivot drills, and empty water bottles that he places strategically on the ground for swing-path drills. These are only part of his homemade stash of training aids, and we haven't even spotted him practicing on the putting green yet! Vijay also uses commercially manufactured training aids that anyone can purchase at a well-stocked golf shop.

Not only does alternating between drills and shots improve your swing dynamics, it also makes your practice sessions diversified and fun. What's more, the breaks you take between hitting shots and drilling require you to adjust to a new target when you return to hitting balls. In other words, firing twenty-seven 8-irons in a row off into the atmosphere, without any target in mind, may be good physical exercise, but it hardly qualifies as golf practice. Creating diversity during your practice sessions, however, mirrors how you play the game on the golf course, as each and every shot you face presents itself as a unique situation that requires you to come up with a creative solution.

I've always striven to keep practice creative and fun, and I can honestly say that I've never been bored on the practice range. With so many aspects of the game, and so many ways to practice them creatively, being bored just isn't in golf's equation, as far as I'm concerned.

I encourage you to invent your own drills and practice exercises that ingrain your dynamics in your mind, and to swing in your own personal way. For example, here's one Andy Brumer came up with for the straight plane line Dynamic Number Five.

Go to the practice green during the middle of the day when the sun is shining, and find the shadow line cast by one of the green's flagsticks. Place a ball right on that line, and then address it with a midiron, so that you are standing perpendicular to the line. The shadow line with the ball on it represents your straight plane line. Now, take a slow-motion swing, and observe the shadow of your club head as it swings through the impact zone. You will clearly see how the club head approaches the ball from inside the shadow line, but nevertheless *points directly at it*. The club head only touches the line when the club hits the ball, before returning immediately inside the line, on-plane, after impact. The club head, in essence, draws a circular arc right through the impact zone, while it points to the straight plane line throughout.

Now, purposely try to swing the club head directly over the shadow line, rather than approaching it from inside of it. Now you can clearly see that the shadow of your shaft points across, or beyond, the straight plane line, indicating that you have swung off-plane through the impact zone. This drill very graphically illustrates the fact that an on-plane swing finds the club pointing to the plane line throughout the entire impact zone, while only touching it when the club meets the ball, and that an overly conscious and forced attempt to *trace* or cover the line, throws the club incorrectly over the plane line.

Many people have told me that they have given up golf because they just don't have time to practice. Certainly, it's great fun to spend leisurely hours working at your game at a quality grass driving range, but you can also improve your swing dynamics in just five minutes a day. In fact, that's what I did back in 2000, when I was preparing to qualify for the U.S. Open at Pebble Beach (which I succeeded in doing!). Busy with my TV work for CBS, my golf design business, church and charity work, not to mention family obligations, I nevertheless committed myself to five minutes a day to swinging a club in a variety of contexts and circumstances, or I could putt, chip, and pitch at the golf course's practice green for fifteen minutes if I didn't have time to hit a bucket of balls, with the goal of improving my dynamics clearly in my mind.

Often, during a break in the action during my son Daniel's soccer games, I'd take a club out of the car and go behind the bleachers, where there is decent grass, and take practice swings, monitoring my divots, as I do during the sand drill. When I was in college, I cut a cup-size hole in the carpet in my apartment to work on my putting; and, while I had to replace the carpet when I moved out, the improvement in my flat-left-wrist alignment at impact, while putting, was well worth the cost. You can keep the matting knife in the drawer, and improve the speed of your putting at home by stroking the ball to a quarter on the carpet and trying to make the ball stop about eighteen inches past the coin.

When I played the PGA Tour full-time, I'd often choose which hotels I'd book rooms in, based on how closely the room's carpet resembled a Tour-quality putting green (I sometimes still do so today, though I'm not sure my wife, Marianna, who sometimes travels with me, would want to hear this!). During the 2000 U.S. Open, the house I rented on the Monterey Peninsula had a nice, sandy driveway, and—you guessed it—it became my sand drill space, where I worked on my forward swing bottom dynamic for five-minute sessions throughout the week.

Now I'd like to clarify some murky thinking about preround practice. People say that it's important to get to the golf course early to warm up on the practice tee before you begin your round. Well, I agree with the first thought, i.e., to budget in some time for preround practice, but I don't believe your time spent on the practice tee should ever be for the purpose of warming up. After all, they call it the practice range, not the warm-up range, for good reason.

So, if your course doesn't have a small gym or exercise room where you can warm up appropriately on a stationary bike or treadmill, stand on the back of the range and do a series of stretching exercises and brisk-walking, in-place steps, to get your heart rate up, then go to your hitting bay and work on your swing a bit before teeing off. In other words, by the time you hit your first practice shot on the range, whether before playing a round of golf or on a practice-only day, you should be sufficiently warm enough to start working on your swing dynamics.

I have found that it takes me about twenty-five full practice swings to reach this point, or about ten minutes. Pay attention to how many practice swings you need to sufficiently warm up your body.

Let's return to the subject of a varied practice session. Another reason you want to mix drills with hitting actual shots at alternate targets is, that hitting too many balls in succession makes you too ball-conscious. Now, rather than using your aiming point technique to produce a forward swing bottom, you fix your attention on the back of the ball, which moves your swing bottom rearward, rather than forward, of the ball. In other words, hitting too many balls in a row is a *hypnotic* rather than a *dynamic* way to practice!

Not long ago, I spoke with Tom Lehman about practice. He said he had fallen into the habit of hitting too many balls on the range, and that his swing was not getting better because of it. He solved the problem by practicing on the course, playing two balls per hole. Whether practicing or playing in a tournament, Tom also likes to execute drills and make practice swings between hitting his shots, which you can often see him do on a televised event.

Phil Mickelson's somewhat unusual practice routine before a major tournament sometimes involves going to a course other than the event's venue (usually with his short game teacher, Dave Pelz, and his full swing coach, Rick Smith, in tow) and working on his game there, before the competition begins. Phil wants to place himself as closely as possible into a playing mode on days leading up to a major tournament, and he feels that removing himself from the media, the bleachers, the fans, and even his fellow pros—many of whom treat practice days in a more low-keyed fashion than when the competition begins—lets him do this. What's more, practicing on a new course this way sharpens Phil's senses, and requires him to interact with the golf course in a very focused way.

Phil understands that, in addition to hitting balls on the range, he has to *practice playing the game on the golf course as well.* That playing itself requires practice is a lesson all of us who tend to become too comfortable hitting balls on the driving range should learn.

T

THE DYNO-METER: TURNING IT ON AS I SIGN OFF FROM THE IMPACT ZONE

As this chapter draws to an end—indeed, as I bring this book to its conclusion—I'd like to leave you with a little drill—a game of sorts—that I created with Andy Brumer, which I think will serve as a great tool to help you become your own best coach. The game is called the "Dyno-Meter," and it represents a kind of biological version of a computerized launch monitor. Whereas an actual launch monitor focuses its lenses or sensors on the impact zone, to record a shot's launch angle, spin rate, direction, and ball speed, the Dyno-Meter subjectively records each swing's dynamics. The best thing about this no-tech device is that it's completely invisible! It exists in your brain, your imagination, your hands, and your capacity to sense how dynamically (or not) you struck each practice shot.

The Dyno-Meter is simple and fun to operate, and it works in the following way: Go ahead and hit a shot, a 7-iron, let's say, and after completed, give that shot a Dyno-Meter rating. A score of ten means that you executed the shot with all of your dynamics working at their highest efficiency, i.e., you struck the ball with a flat left wrist at impact, with a lagging golf club that still retained virtually all its loaded power. You delivered the club head along a straight plane line, through the impact zone, and achieved a forward swing bottom, with a divot whose center was four inches in front of the ball. *Voila!* You found the dynamic Holy Grail of golf . . . on that shot anyway.

A Dyno-Meter reading of zero would tell the story of a very poorly executed swing. On this shot, your divot revealed a swing bottom behind the ball, and an impact that occurred with a cupped or broken-down left wrist, which indicates a loss of lag and load, and an out-to-in swing path that cuts across your straight plane line. Oh, well, no one's perfect.

We can also adjust the Dyno-Meter to grade separate dynamics individually on individual shots. So, let's say you were a little bit awkward on one swing, meaning not so smooth in loading the club on the backswing, therefore the Dyno-Meter would record a score of six for loading. On the next swing, you succeeded in storing *some* lag, but you began to lose it a little too early in the downswing. The Dyno-Meter spurts out a reading of five for lag on that swing.

Of course, you can set the Dyno-Meter to run at its full capacity of both measuring each dynamic individually, and the dynamic efficiency of the swing as a whole. For example, let's say you load the club nicely (which yields a score of nine), and your pivot works fairly well to transport your lag into the impact zone (the Dyno-Meter registers eight for lag), so you strike this shot with a flat left wrist (but not with as firm a wrist as possible, which earns a score of seven for the flat-left-wrist dynamic), and, while you deliver the club along a straight plane line through the impact zone (a solid ten), the center of your divot measures two, rather than four, inches in front of the ball (which merits a six on the Dyno-Meter scale). When you average all of the dynamics' scores together, you receive an eight for that swing. Very good; but you still have a little work to do!

Who knows, maybe someday I'll be commentating over a slow-motion Swing Vision swing on TV, with the Dyno-Meter installed and turned on. "Well Jim, Tiger's Number-Three Dynamic of loading the club on the backswing was very effective on that swing, a solid nine. And he increased his downswing lag angle very nicely (Dynamic Number Four). I'll give him a ten for that. Just look at his flat left wrist at impact (Dynamic Number One), it was so flat that it appeared slightly bowed or arched, which created a significant forward lean of the club shaft of seven degrees! That's a ten in my book, while his divot revealed a forward swing bottom (Dynamic Number Two) of five inches in front of the ball. The Dyno-Meter's showing ten for that one, also, but he started the shot twenty feet right of his target (Dynamic Number Five), so I can only give him a five for that dynamic. His high grades on his first four dynamics meant that he hit a nice, solid shot pin-high. But his low reading on the Fifth Dynamic placed him in a low-percentage place on the green, from which it would be difficult to make birdie, so he'll probably make par."

I'm sure such commentary would get Gary McCord and David Feherty scratching their heads, itching for early retirement! I can hear David now, under the urging of another CBS golf commentator, Verne Lunquist, saying, "Bobby, I didn't realize we were covering the world figure-skating championship and discussing 'technical merit'." Well, maybe the Dyno-Meter won't make it to CBS after all, but it can, from time to time, be a fun and helpful way to monitor your progress, as you work on improving your swing dynamics.

It has been my pleasure, and the pleasure of my writing partner, Andy Brumer, to get you started on a dynamic path to better golf. While the instruction in this book probably won't raise your level of play to that of a Tiger Woods, it will allow you to set the same reachable goal Tiger has set for himself: that of continual improvement. The way Tiger gets better, and the way all of you can do so as well, is by working diligently and patiently on improving your swing dynamics through the impact zone.

BULLET POINTS

- There's a bit of the child left in all of us; therefore, we all have retained an ability to emulate or mimic the good swings we see, and imprint them into our memory bank. Study your favorite tour pros' swings and picture yourself making those dynamic motions yourself.

- It's important that you do not rush the process of improving your dynamics. We live in a society that craves instant gratification and would have us believe that, after reading an instruction article in a golf magazine, by osmosis, the information programs your body to execute that lesson perfectly. But in golf we need patience and discipline, to first absorb, then understand and imagine, the correct swing dynamics, before upgrading them through practice and applying them in actual play.

- People think that all Vijay Singh does is go to the range every day and beat balls for hours on end. Well, you don't become the number-one player in the world, as Vijay did not too long ago, by mindlessly hitting golf balls until your fingers bleed. In fact, Vijay spends as much time doing drills on the range as he does actually hitting balls. For every group of five or six balls he may hit in a row, he'll take a break and spend as much time doing drills. I recommend this fifty-fifty ratio for all golfers.

- Swing style is an expression of swing dynamics, and not the other way around. For example, all dynamic swingers lag a fully loaded club through the impact zone. But different players set or establish this load in a range of styles. Nick Faldo, Corey Pavin, and the promising young PGA Tour player Ryan Moore set the club very early in their backswings, to establish their load. Tiger Woods, Vijay Singh, Luke Donald, and countless others set or load the club gradually, so that, by the middle of their backswings, they have completed the job. Jack Nicklaus, the late Payne Stewart, and Sergio Garcia are among those who set and load the club very late in their backswings.

- I've always striven to keep practice creative and fun, and I can honestly say that I've never been bored on the practice range. With so many aspects of the game, and so many ways to practice them creatively, being bored just isn't in golf 's equation, as far as I'm concerned. I encourage you to invent your own drills and practice exercises that ingrain your dynamics in your mind, and to swing in your own personal way.